Henry Fernandez is a man of faith. I witnessed firsthand the tremendous financial miracles in his ministry. He has a deep passion for instructing God's people on getting out of financial trouble and staying free from debt. I believe this book will be a blessing to all who read it.

—**Dr. Don Colbert**
New York Times best-selling author
and family practice physician

In this book, Henry Fernandez helps readers regain a life that is built on God's foundation. And he gives us practical steps to build on that foundation in order to ultimately discover the amazing design and destination God has in store for us all!

—**Ed Young**
Pastor, Fellowship Church, Grapevine, Texas
Author, *Outrageous, Contagious Joy*

I first met Henry Fernandez in 2010 to discuss the possibility of my accounting firm becoming the new independent auditing firm for his church. One of the first things Henry said to me was, "We want to do everything right. Above reproach. Whatever it takes. No matter what." How refreshing that is in today's culture. If there is a type of person whose advice and wisdom we should heed in the areas of *Faith, Family & Finances*, it is a person with a genuine heart for integrity in all avenues of life.

—**Michael E. Batts**
Author and CPA, Batts, Morrison, Wales & Lee

Fernandez' book carries a great message that urges us to return to our First Love, who will enable us to rebuild everything in our lives that life's storms have torn down.

—**CeCe Winans**
Dove Award-winning recording artist

Faith,
Family &
Finances

Strong Foundations for a Better Life

Henry FERNANDEZ

WHITAKER
HOUSE

Literary development by David W. Bohon/Orchard Media Group

FAITH, FAMILY & FINANCES

Henry Fernandez
P.O. Box 100127
Fort Lauderdale, FL 33310
www.henryfernandez.org

ISBN: 978-1-60374-280-1
Printed in the United States of America
© 2012 by Henry Fernandez

Whitaker House
1030 Hunt Valley Circle
New Kensington, PA 15068
www.whitakerhouse.com

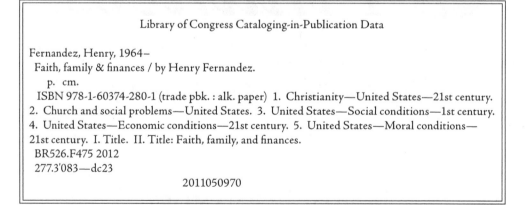

Library of Congress Cataloging-in-Publication Data

Fernandez, Henry, 1964–
  Faith, family & finances / by Henry Fernandez.
    p. cm.
  ISBN 978-1-60374-280-1 (trade pbk. : alk. paper) 1. Christianity—United States—21st century.
2. Church and social problems—United States. 3. United States—Social conditions—1st century.
4. United States—Economic conditions—21st century. 5. United States—Moral conditions—
21st century. I. Title. II. Title: Faith, family, and finances.
  BR526.F475 2012
  277.3'083—dc23
                        2011050970

1 2 3 4 5 6 7 8 9 10 11   19 18 17 16 15 14 13 12

Foreword

Anyone can have a theory. God has a plan! Seeking Him and His Word to discover that plan is the kingdom of God's way to success in life. Jesus said it like this: *"Seek ye first the kingdom of God, and his righteousness; and all these things shall be added unto you"* (Matthew 6:33 KJV).

Henry and Carol Fernandez set out a number of years ago to seek first that plan and to put it into action. Henry is not a man with a theory but a man of faith with the plan, accompanied by the success that goes along with it. *Faith, Family & Finances* is the product of living it before you teach it. Henry and Carol have been there when only faith in God's Word and His way of doing things could deliver them. I have known them long enough to observe their faith in action and to see them triumph in Christ Jesus against all odds.

This God-anointed, brilliantly written book will, along with God's Word, help you to get back on track to having a steadfast faith in God and His Word, a strong family, and a stable financial life that is separate from the world's failing system.

Don't just read this book; study it, along with your Bible. Compare each word with Scripture. Once you are sure that it does not represent what someone else thinks or what someone says the Bible says, then, put it into action. *Faith, Family & Finances* will teach you exactly how that's done. Become a doer of the Word, and not just a hearer only. (See James 1:22.) Get ready for the Lord Jesus Christ to manifest Himself to you and lead you into His plan. *"I have come that they may have life, and that they may have it more abundantly"* (John 10:10).

Jesus is Lord!

—Kenneth Copeland
Founder, Kenneth Copeland Ministries, Fort Worth, Texas

Contents

Introduction:
Returning to Strong Faith,
Families, and Finances

If the foundations are destroyed, what can the righteous
do?   (Psalm 11:3)

This passage of Scripture gives us the following warning: If God's foundations for order and success are destroyed, to whom or to what are good people to turn?

I believe that, in these present days, we are reaping the consequences of the destruction of godly standards that are crucial to our success as individuals and as a nation. Only by returning to God's standards in every area of life will we once again begin to enjoy the blessings He has promised His children.

While the financial crisis that America has faced over these last few years seemed to hit many people and communities out of the blue, I must confess that I had witnessed the ominous economic and social storm clouds brewing for several years, and I felt a growing concern for the many individuals and families who would be directly and adversely impacted.

In greater Fort Lauderdale, Florida, where I pastor a multicultural congregation of several thousand families, I became alarmed as I detected a selfish mind-set that seemed to be growing throughout the community. A self-centered spirit appeared to be taking root in the hearts and minds of the people, an attitude that drove them to pursue riches and success, to run after recreation and leisure, while giving less and less thought to the solid foundations of faith, family, and financial stewardship—the very things that help ensure strong, healthy individuals and communities.

Casting Off Restraint

Where there is no revelation, the people cast off restraint;
but happy is he who keeps the law.   (Proverbs 29:18)

As I observed these self-centered attitudes spreading all around me, this verse came to mind. It says, in effect, "When people begin to ignore the guidance that God has given them for their own good, self-restraint goes out the window, and they begin to run wild." This is what I sensed happening in my community and across the nation. Restraint was out the window, and we were headed toward certain crisis.

On the surface, the nation seemed to be riding a wave of economic prosperity. Jobs were plentiful, industries and businesses were booming, and abundance blossomed everywhere. Because of this façade of plenty, people were living with little thought for tomorrow and placing few limits, if any, on their budgets, their time, or their desires. People were borrowing, spending, living, and planning as if prosperity and abundance were their birthrights. I watched as young families borrowed money to purchase homes, automobiles, and luxury items that seemed to far exceed their financial means. Businesses expanded and took risks with the expectation that the economic upturn would last forever. Across America, people's appetites for "the good life" appeared to be unending.

By mid-September 2008, however, things came to a screeching halt as banks, lenders, and other long-respected financial institutions considered "too big to fail" collapsed, almost overnight. On September 15, the Dow Jones Industrial Average lost a historic 504 points, and, over the next several weeks, hundreds of billions of dollars evaporated from pension funds, retirement accounts, and 401(k) plans. Where optimism had once flourished, fear took over as the dreams of a life of ease and luxury began to melt away.

Since that time, America has watched as prestigious companies—businesses that at one time helped to make America the industrial giant of the world—teetered on the edge of bankruptcy.

The federal government was forced to intervene in an effort to shore up a national economy that seemed on the verge of collapse.

Faith is reacting positively to a negative situation.
—Dr. Robert Schuller

Returning to God's Blueprint

Since that time, I have spoken with and counseled an unending trail of individuals who have lost jobs, homes, dreams, and, in many cases, the very will to go on. Janis is one of these people. She wrote to tell me her story:

This past May marked my fifth month out of work. I've been living only on unemployment benefits, which isn't much. I owed my landlord over $3100, and June was almost here. Each month, I get my unemployment check, pay my tithes to God, and give as much of the rest as I can to him so that he knows I am trying. Throughout this time, I have been putting all my trust and faith in the Lord that everything would work out. In May, however, my landlord called to say that I needed to start figuring out what I was going to do because he needs to make money from his property. I understood that, but, because of the God I serve, I confidently told him that by the end of the month, I would have all of what I owed him, plus June's rent, as well.

—Janis

There are many others in situations similar to Janis's. "Bishop Fernandez," they tell me, "I have trusted God and lived the life I thought I was supposed to live, and now, everything He has blessed me with is disappearing. What happened? Where did I go wrong? How do I pick up the pieces and get back on the right track? Are God's blessings gone forever? Will I ever see His blessings again in my life?"

If you are struggling with questions like these, if you feel that God has abandoned you, or if you fear that the life you worked so long to build is gone forever, I have good news: the

I have good news: the God who created you has a master blueprint for your life that includes abundance for today and for all your tomorrows.

God who created you has a master blueprint for your life that includes abundance for today and for all your tomorrows.

The problem is that too many individuals and families have traded God's blueprint for one of their own making. In other words, they have allowed the foundations of righteousness in their lives to become compromised. What do I mean by that? Where they once trusted in God and put Him first in their lives, little by little, they subtly began to trust in other things—careers, jobs, education, or government—for their provision and significance. Their faith in God was nudged to the back burner. In the process, they slowly allowed other important issues of life to suffer, as well. Perhaps the health of their marriage took second place to a pursuit of the "American Dream." Perhaps, little time remained for proper parenting, and even their children became like strangers to them.

If this scenario sounds at all familiar, I want you to hear something: it is not too late to turn things around and become the kind of individual, family, community, and nation that God can bless and use for His glory once again.

There are three keys to doing this, and I will deal with each of them specifically in this book. They are:

- Returning to strong faith in God and His Word
- Returning strength and stability to the family
- Returning to wise financial stewardship based on God's counsel

God has given us sound, fail-safe counsel for each of these keys. That is what this book is all about. In Janis's case, I believe that her financial faithfulness to God, even during times of crisis, made all the difference.

Yesterday, May 23, I received a phone call informing me that I had won eight thousand dollars in a court settlement. I started dancing around the house and praising God because I knew this was from Him.

When I picked up my settlement money, I took out a tithe, sent my landlord all the money I owed him, plus my rent for June, and I am now paying my other outstanding bills. This is what I had been praying for; I had asked God for a "right now" blessing, as only He can give, and as only He did give. Hallelujah!

As you read the simple but profound counsel of God contained in the following chapters, remember that change happens one step at a time. Rebuilding righteous standards in your faith, your family, and your finances begins by responding to the signposts God has placed along your path. As you follow His leading, confessing and repenting of your sins and missteps, changing your direction as you trust in His Word and promises, and following His plans for success, you will discover blessings, abundance, and richness in every area of your life.

God's promises and plans for you are the same as they have always been—He never changes. I am excited to hear from you as you follow His blueprint for success.

Part I:

FAITH

I am inwardly fashioned for faith, not for fear. Fear is not my native land; faith is. I am so made that worry and anxiety are sand in the machinery of life; faith is the oil. I live better by faith and confidence than by fear, doubt, and anxiety. In anxiety and worry, my being is gasping for breath—these are not my native air. But in faith and confidence, I breathe freely—these are my native air.

—Dr. E. Stanley Jones
Author and evangelist

Chapter One

In Whom Do You Trust?

"In God We Trust." That is a powerful declaration, isn't it? Although we seldom notice it, that solemn and weighty phrase graces every unit of American currency, from the lowly penny to the $100 bill. It's not merely a slogan or a nice sentiment that we intone on holidays or in times of national crisis. There is meaning and intent behind those words. "In God We Trust" is based on the conviction, held by generations of Americans since the nation's founding, that a country and its citizens are only as strong as their faith in, and faithfulness to, almighty God.

That, of course, is God's opinion on the matter, as well. Throughout the annals of history, He has promised to bless those nations and people who put their trust in Him, corporately and individually, and who behave in ways that honor Him and His character. By contrast, He has clearly warned that those who do not reverence and put their trust in Him can expect to suffer physically, financially, emotionally, and politically—in every way imaginable!

Blessed is the nation whose God is the LORD, the people He has chosen as His own inheritance. (Psalm 33:12)

A Look to the Past

Look at America's past and you will see that, for the majority of our history, we have been the nation to which other nations have looked for guidance, help, defense, and a model of a successful, prosperous society. There is good reason for this.

For most of the past two centuries, we have been the most pros-perous and successful nation on earth. Consider the following:

- The lion's share of technological advances that occurred during the twentieth century—from automobiles to elec-tric lights to television and radio to the computer and space travel—had their start in America.

- During this same time, America's industrial machine was second to none, pumping out volumes of manufactured goods for markets all over the world.

- For most of that time, America was also blessed with re-markable agricultural production, an abundance that has been used to feed not only our own sizeable and ever-growing population but also that of many other nations of the world.

- Our educational institutions were world renowned, rais-ing generations of young people who were trained not only with life skills to succeed in business, industry, and else-where, but also with the precepts of righteousness and morality that are the foundation of any successful society.

Without a doubt, the greatest asset of America's blessedness has been its people. In America, God has brought together in-dividuals, families, and communities from a wide variety of for-eign countries, cultures, ethnicities, and races, forming a veri-table "melting pot" of hardworking, moral, and God-honoring people who asked for nothing more in return than the opportu-nity to be an integral part of this "land of the free and home of the brave."

Committed to a solid faith in God, to strong families, and to earnest stewardship of all that God had blessed them with, this broad range of individuals built strong communities "from sea to shining sea" so that, for generations to come, our country could declare that America was "one nation under God."

Throughout the years, as long as Americans have trusted in God, they have maintained that same strength and unity, enabling them to achieve just about anything they set their minds and hearts to do.

The secret of my success? It is simple. It is found in the
Bible: *"In all thy ways acknowledge him, and he shall
direct thy paths."* —George Washington Carver

A Change of Heart

Today, however, many people are wondering what has happened to our strong, free nation that once put its trust in God.
The cultural landscape around us, and the personal circumstances millions of Americans are facing, seem far different
from the prosperity, security, and hope that so many of us grew
up with. The list of challenges is daunting.

- The nation's job picture is bleak. As of August 2011, unemployment was 9.1 percent, with nearly fourteen million Americans out of work. How different from the nation
  in which previous generations raised their families and
  planned for the future.

- Over the last thirty years, more and more Americans have
  gone into debt for nonessential luxury items. As of January 2010, Americans held more than 609 billion credit
  cards—or two cards for every American. In June 2011,
  U.S. consumer credit card debt reached $793 billion, with
  an average credit card debt per household of $15,799.[1]
  What a difference from the practice of thrift that previous
  generations of Americans have displayed.

- With so many Americans in so much debt, it's little surprise that in 2010, filings for personal bankruptcy exploded to more than 1.5 million people.[2]

- On the housing front, where home ownership was once
  a carefully considered decision for previous generations,
  over the last several years, it has become an entitlement.
  Untold millions of Americans have gone into debt for
  homes whose mortgages far exceeded their incomes. As of
  July 2011, the national foreclosure rate had come down
  to 1 in every 111 homes, a 29 percent drop from the first
  half of 2010. In my own state of Florida, however, the rate

was still among the nation's worst with 14 percent of all homes actively in foreclosure.[3]

- As the economy has faltered and families have lost their homes, homelessness has become a national epidemic. According to a 2007 study by the National Law Center on Homelessness and Poverty, approximately 3.5 million individuals in America are now homeless—1.35 million of them children.[4]

- Just as the economy in crisis has impacted individuals, families, and communities, it has also devastated businesses and financial institutions. Long-established, respected banks, investment companies, and lending institutions—many considered "too big to fail"—have collapsed, while others have survived only through the direct intervention of a government that is being increasingly stressed in its ability to provide the answers.

Family and Morality: A Changing Landscape

Destroy the family, and you destroy the country.
—Vladimir Ilyich Lenin

The essential building block of any society is the family, and American society is no exception. From its beginning, strong families living morally upright lives have been an important ingredient to a strong America. We may snicker or roll our eyes at the straight-laced values from thirty, forty, or fifty years ago, but the truth is that life certainly seemed simpler and more wholesome back then.

Families, whatever the faults and foibles of their members, were stronger and more stable. Marriage was considered to be a sacred institution. There were stricter standards that governed relationships between the sexes, children were more

From its beginning, strong families living morally upright lives have been an important ingredient to a strong America.

respectful of their elders, and the values that defined behavior in society tended to keep people on the straight and narrow.

That seems to be far from the case today:

- In many sectors of our society, marriage has become an option rather than a sacred trust. A study by the National Marriage Project found that cohabitation—couples living together outside the bond of marriage—has become so accepted in our society that an increasing number of Americans view it as a perfectly functional alternative to marriage. Their study quoted U.S. Census figures, which claimed that in 1997, there were more than four million unmarried couples sharing a household, up from less than a half million in 1960.[5] A study conducted by the Institute for Social Research at the University of Michigan found that nearly two in five children will spend at least some time living with a parent and an unmarried partner.[6]

- With such a casual approach to lifelong relationships, it is no wonder that the institution of marriage seems to be in absolute crisis throughout America. A recent study by the Barna Group found that one out of three Americans who has been married has also been divorced. As George Barna noted in the study, "There no longer seems to be much of a stigma attached to divorce; it is now seen as an unavoidable rite of passage."[7]

- Along with a drastic increase in divorce has come a wholesale redefinition of what marriage means in America. Several states have ruled that marriage can no longer be defined as only between a man and a woman. In some states, unions between two men or two women have been declared legally acceptable. One wonders if there will be any end to the redefinition of God's most foundational building block for humanity.

- Over the last thirty-five-plus years, children have become increasingly vulnerable to neglect and, in many cases, an inconvenience to people's freewheeling lifestyles. The fact that, since 1973, over forty million precious babies have met their deaths through abortion represents a serious blight on our nation.

What Has Happened to Our Faith?

In April 2009, during a trip to Turkey, President Barack Obama held a press conference in which he said, "One of the great strengths of the United States is—although as I mentioned, we have a very large Christian population, we do not consider ourselves a Christian nation or a Jewish nation or a Muslim nation; we consider ourselves a nation of citizens who are bound by ideals and a set of values."[8] If that statement by the leader of our nation does not seem alarming, recall that in June 2006, Mr. Obama delivered a speech to the Call for Renewal Conference, sponsored by the progressive Christian magazine *Sojourners*, in which his prepared remarks stated, "Whatever we once were, we are no longer just a Christian nation; we are also a Jewish nation, a Muslim nation, a Buddhist nation, a Hindu nation, and a nation of nonbelievers."[9]

Now, in one sense, President Obama is right. America was never intended to be a nation where individuals were compelled to become Christians. One of the great values of our nation is that everyone has the freedom to worship God after the dictates of his or her own heart.

Nevertheless, whatever the president meant by his statements, the undeniable truth of the matter is that America was established upon Christian precepts, and it seems that, as a nation and a people, we have drifted away from those foundations. As a consequence, we are now paying a price that only repentance and turning back to God will cure.

More than two hundred years ago, another president made a very different declaration. At his first inauguration, George Washington reminded his fellow citizens:

No people can be bound to acknowledge and adore the invisible hand, which conducts the Affairs of men more than the People of the United States. Every step, by which they have advanced to the character of an independent nation, seems to have been distinguished by some token of providential agency....We ought to be no less persuaded that the propitious smiles of Heaven, can never be expected on a nation that disregards the eternal rules of order and right, which Heaven itself has ordained.[10]

God Himself reminds us in the Bible that upright, godly Christian living will make and keep a nation and a people great. By contrast, sin, rebellion, selfishness, greed, and turning away from God and His Word will bring reproach and, ultimately, destruction.

Righteousness exalts a nation, but sin is a reproach to any people. (Proverbs 14:34)

The Foundation for Success

Now, I realize that the America of today is far different from the one President Washington addressed so many years ago. In fact, many individuals living in the United States are not even American citizens, and they may have difficulty identifying with the values and culture that have defined our country over many generations. The fact remains, however, that the beliefs, behaviors, attitudes, and actions of a specific group of people inhabiting a place—whether it is two people or more than 300 million people—will largely determine whether those people will live in peace, health, abundance, security, and plenty, or in constant turmoil, danger, poverty, disease, and lack.

Now it shall come to pass, if you diligently obey the voice of the LORD your God, to observe carefully all His commandments which I command you today, that the LORD your God will set you high above all nations of the earth. And all these blessings shall come upon you and overtake you, because you obey the voice of the LORD your

God: Blessed shall you be in the city, and blessed shall you be in the country. Blessed shall be the fruit of your body, the produce of your ground and the increase of your herds, the increase of your cattle and the offspring of your flocks. Blessed shall be your basket and your kneading bowl. Blessed shall you be when you come in, and blessed shall you be when you go out. The LORD will cause your enemies who rise against you to be defeated before your face; they shall come out against you one way and flee before you seven ways. The LORD will command the blessing on you in your storehouses and in all to which you set your hand, and He will bless you in the land which the LORD your God is giving you. The LORD will establish you as a holy people to Himself, just as He has sworn to you, if you keep the commandments of the LORD your God and walk in His ways. Then all peoples of the earth shall see that you are called by the name of the LORD, and they shall be afraid of you. And the LORD will grant you plenty of goods, in the fruit of your body, in the increase of your livestock, and in the produce of your ground, in the land of which the LORD swore to your fathers to give you. The LORD will open to you His good treasure, the heavens, to give the rain to your land in its season, and to bless all the work of your hand. You shall lend to many nations, but you shall not borrow. And the LORD will make you the head and not the tail; you shall be above only, and not be beneath, if you heed the commandments of the LORD your God, which I command you today, and are careful to observe them.

(Deuteronomy 28:1–13)

When God called the nation of Israel to be His own special people, He promised to be with them, to guide them, and to bless them with perfect health, overwhelming abundance for their every need, the favor of the people and nations around them, and success in whatever they set their hands to do. He told them that His blessings would overtake them and that they would not be able to stop the favor of God upon their lives. All they had to do was trust Him, put Him first over everything else, and follow the directions He gave them for life.

Unfortunately, God's people often ended up doing the exact opposite, and they paid a painful price. Their disobedience—their lack of trust in God's mercy and goodness, and their insistence on looking to their own faulty wisdom and planning rather than to God's perfect blueprint for their lives—sometimes led them, throughout their long history, to be in bondage to other nations. Throughout all of their ordeals, God continued to call His people back to His perfect path, where blessings and abundance awaited them.

That story may sound familiar. It is much like the situations and circumstances that we face today. We say a little prayer, hoping for God's blessing, and then we forge ahead with our own plans and agendas rather than waiting for His perfect timing. Although we are well aware of God's counsel, too many of us end up following the opposite course of action. Of course, gentleman that He is, God allows us to go our own way, patiently waiting for us to come to the end of ourselves, where we finally say, "Father, I was wrong; You were right. Take control."

> **God is waiting for a decision by each one of us to turn from our own ways—with all the heartache and turmoil attached to them—and return to His perfect way.**

That is what God is waiting for: a decision by each one of us to turn from our own ways—with all the heartache and turmoil attached to them—and return to His perfect way. He promises in His Word that He will wait until we are ready to receive His mercy, when we have come to the end of ourselves and our own resources, our own ideas and strategies, so that we can rest instead in His care, receive His salvation, and feast at His table of plenty.

For thus says the Lord God, the Holy One of Israel: "In returning and rest you shall be saved; in quietness and

confidence shall be your strength." But you would not....
Therefore the LORD will wait, that He may be gracious to
you; and therefore He will be exalted, that He may have
mercy on you. For the LORD is a God of justice; blessed
are all those who wait for Him.   (Isaiah 30:15, 18)

Returning to the God of Our Salvation

It certainly seems that a dramatic shift is taking place within our own nation and, indeed, throughout the world. The prosperity, abundance, plenty, and peace that have been assumed as our right and privilege for so long now appear to be drifting away. In their place has come an abundance of uncertainty, even fear, about the future.

Jobs that once seemed plentiful and secure are rare and disappearing. Financial resources that seemed so abundant a few years ago now are scarce or nonexistent. The peace, order, and beauty of many of our neighborhoods and communities are being replaced by violence, abuse, corruption, decay, crime, and chaos. Many of our homes, once sanctuaries of peace against the slings and arrows of the cold workaday world, have become disordered, discordant and abusive. The laughter and happiness of many of our children, once secure and well-adjusted, have been replaced, in many cases, by rebellion, anger, pride, and disobedience. Loving couples, committed to each other "till death us do part," have been replaced to a large degree by "partners," devoted more to self and the pursuit of pleasure than to the welfare of the other, with discord, separation, and divorce as the fruit of their unions.

> **God has a promise for each individual—and every collective people—who will turn to Him in humility and absolute trust.**

Is there hope for a nation and a people who once declared unashamedly "In God We Trust" but who are now mired in sin and selfish living, and who are drifting and confused? The answer is an emphatic and unequivocal "Yes!" God has a promise for each individual—and every collective people—who will turn to Him in humility and absolute trust. Just as He told His people, Israel, He still says to you and me, *"Only in return-ing to me and resting in me will you be saved. In quietness and confidence is your strength"* (Isaiah 30:15 NLT).

To many of us, that may sound like a tall order, an impos-sible feat to accomplish. When everything within us is scream-ing, in our need and anxiety, *Don't just stand there and trust God! Do something; anything!,* to choose to be still and trust God seems almost ridiculous. But believe me, God is right there to help you, to enable you to stand and wait for Him through the power of His Holy Spirit. He is not far away but near to each of us in our need.

Anything less than God will let you down.

—E. Stanley Jones

Are You That Individual?

Whatever your need today, God is waiting to meet it, out of His mercy. He is looking for individuals who will make faith and a relationship with Him a lifestyle. He is looking for people who will be part of a worldwide community of believers who turn their families, neighborhoods, communities, and nations back to God. He is searching for those who will stand in the gap, committed to a strong and vital faith; for those who will build strong families who trust God together; and for those who will practice financial stewardship based on godly, scriptural principles.

The turnaround for a nation and a people on the brink be-gins with one person saying "Yes!" to God. Are you just such an individual? In the following chapters, I will show how you can find a doorway to the kind of faith that can move mount-ains in your life—mountains and obstacles you may have long thought would block God's blessings forever. I will also show you God's counsel on building strong families that can weather any storm life throws at them. Finally, I will show you God's perfect counsel on sound finances—something all of us need in these days of uncertainty.

Be assured, God's provision—and all His best for you—is not dependent upon the economy, the whims of the stock market, how much money you have in the bank, or if you have a job tomorrow. God's provision for you and your family is dependent upon one thing alone: God's faithfulness to His Word. He is the Creator of everything—all the wealth of the world is at His command—and He has promised to supply all your needs according to all the riches of His glorious and unending kingdom. (See Philippians 4:19.)

All you have to do is believe and receive.

Chapter Two

It's All About Relationship

There are certain age-old questions that have been asked by individuals like you and me since the beginning of time:

"Who am I?"

"Why was I born?"

"Is there a reason I am on this earth?"

The ways in which these questions are framed may be endless, but the basic query that each of us must come to grips with boils down to our individual purpose in life. Why are we on this big and often confusing planet called Earth?

Sadly, many people struggle throughout their entire lives and never truly come to grips with their purpose for being here. Others take their cues from those around them, attempting to find the answer in a career, in building a business, or in making money. Others pour their lives into education and the endless pursuit of learning. Still others invest themselves in relationships and family, convinced that these pursuits are where they will find purpose and meaning. Some people think they will find true purpose in philanthropic endeavors, giving of themselves in sacrifice for others. The renowned American psychologist and philosopher William James once said, "The great use of life is to spend it for something that will outlast it." While that sounds noble and good, I am convinced that this kind of thinking misses the point for which you and I were born.

King Solomon, one of the wisest men who ever lived, had an opportunity to experience all the highs and lows that life can bring. While God had given him an incredible gift of wisdom to make the best decisions for both himself and the people he ruled over, Solomon abandoned this precious gift later in life and began to seek after all the luxuries, riches, and sensual extremes that the world had to offer. In Ecclesiastes, he explained that anything he saw and wanted, he pursued wholeheartedly, worked hard to get, or embraced aggressively. His attitude was not much different from that of many people today, working hard, playing hard, and seeking after all the enjoyment and pleasures life has to offer. But let's look at the end result of Solomon's desires.

> *Anything I wanted, I would take. I denied myself no pleasure. I even found great pleasure in hard work, a reward for all my labors. But as I looked at everything I had worked so hard to accomplish, it was all so meaningless—like chasing the wind. There was nothing really worthwhile anywhere.* (Ecclesiastes 2:10–11 NLT)

When he came to the end of his life, Solomon looked back on all he had accomplished, measured all the wealth he had accumulated, and took stock of all the earthly pleasures he had enjoyed. Then, he came to the conclusion that there was only one thing in life that really mattered: knowing God and following Him with abandon.

Saint Augustine, who, like Solomon, allowed himself to experience all the debauchery, sin, and extreme behaviors the world had to offer, came to a conclusion that mirrors Solomon's: "You have made us for Yourself, O Lord, and our hearts are restless until they rest in You."

You Were Created for a Purpose

As I observe the endless frenzy of activities that so many individuals are involved in, I am struck by the restless energy with which so many of us fill our days, always looking for some purpose that will give us a sense of satisfaction and personal fulfillment. Solomon told us that we will search in vain for our life's purpose until we find it in the One who created us: almighty God.

Everything is meaningless—like chasing the wind....So
I decided there is nothing better than to enjoy food and
drink and to find satisfaction in work. Then I realized
that these pleasures are from the hand of God. For who
can eat or enjoy anything apart from him? God gives
wisdom, knowledge, and joy to those who please him.
(Ecclesiastes 2:17, 24–26 NLT)

In a day and age when so many individuals are asking
"What's in it for me?" the idea that we were created for a purpose other than self-fulfillment might seem strange and foreign. But believe me when I tell you that God did not create you
to spend your life acquiring wealth, power, education, relationships, or anything else under the sun. No, He created you for
one purpose, a purpose that is identified in this Scripture:

You are worthy, O Lord, to receive glory and honor and
power; for You created all things, and by Your will they
exist and were created.   (Revelation 4:11)

Take a good look at that statement. The apostle John, one
of the chief leaders of the early church, wrote this foundational statement that has defined the Christian faith through the
ages. You and I—as well as everything else that exists in this
world—were created by the will of God. In fact, today and every
day, you and I continue to exist only because it is God's will.
Such a truth ought to cause you immediately to take stock of
what you are spending your life on. Another translation of this
same Bible verse says that we were created for God's pleasure:
"For thou hast created all things, and for thy pleasure they are
and were created" (KJV). That's right. You and I were created to
give pleasure to God.

Let me ask you a question: Do you feel that your life brings
pleasure to God? How much time during your day do you spend
thinking about how you can make sure God is pleased with
your life? I know of a man who begins each day with the following prayer in his heart and mind: "Lord, I am not going to
spend my day pursuing anything except that which makes You

happy and brings You joy. My first priority is to make sure that You are having a good day!"

What Makes God Happy?

What would happen if you spent your day with that kind of an attitude? Maybe you don't know what it is that makes God happy. How can you even find out? I have good news for you. God has given each of us clear instruction for living a life that brings Him joy and, in the process, gives us unending joy, prosperity, and abundance in every area of life. These instructions are found in His holy Word, the Bible.

> God has given each of us clear instruction for living a life that brings Him joy and, in the process, gives us unending joy, prosperity, and abundance in every area of life.

The problem for many of us is that, instead of opening this book of infinite truth, light, and wisdom in order to find out how to live in a manner that is pleasing to God, we are all too eager to go it alone, trying vainly to find our way using our own wisdom, the ideas of others, or pure guesswork. The harder we try, the more lost and confused we seem to get, and the more deeply entrenched we find ourselves in error and chaos. But it doesn't have to be that way.

Total Trust

The overarching message that God has given to us throughout His Word provides a simple answer as to what makes God happy, and it is this: God is happy when we put our full and total trust in Him.

One of my favorite verses in Proverbs offers this promise of God's never-ending guidance and sustaining power in our lives:

> *Trust in the LORD with all your heart; do not depend on your own understanding. Seek his will in all you do, and*

he will show you which path to take.

(Proverbs 3:5–6 NLT)

Tell me something: How often in your day-to-day life can you say that you trust in the Lord with all your heart? When you are facing serious decisions, or when hardships are knocking on your door, do you suspend *"your own understanding"* and trust instead in God's unfailing Word and in the enduring mercy that He has promised? Can you honestly say that the decisions you make in life are based on acknowledging God as your Source and Provider, and that you are committed to following wherever He leads?

Too often, those of us who have given our lives to Christ and are making an effort to trust Him and live by His Word find ourselves compromising the elements of faith to which we have been called. After all, we live in a world that constantly beckons us to follow the path of least resistance, to do the corrupt things that seem to work for others, and to follow the crowd in what *"seems right"* (Proverbs 14:12). But when we do that, little by little, our faith in God begins to wear down, and we begin to compromise on small issues of faith, trusting God less and less about our finances, our careers, our relationships, our families, and all the nuts and bolts of life. Before long, we discover that what started out as a little compromise is tearing our lives apart.

As God's people, we are called to be different, to live differently than the world lives. The Bible calls us *"a peculiar people"* (1 Peter 2:9 KJV). That's right—we're a little strange. When you decide to trust God fully and completely in every aspect of life, your friends, associates, and even family members might just begin to look at you like you've lost your mind as they witness you making life decisions based on your trust in His Word rather than in worldly wisdom.

As our nation's economy has tightened and the moral climate of our society has become more and more unstable, I truly believe that God is beginning to use these circumstances to call His people to greater faith in Him and away from a world system destined to collapse. In fact, He is calling us to cast off the way the rest of the world lives and to live by a standard of holiness and faith. He doesn't want His children defiled and sullied by the corrupt and unclean mind-set of the world. The world says, "Make your own way, whatever the cost, and you will succeed." But the way of faith, the way that makes God happy, says, *"Trust in the LORD with all your heart, and lean not on your own understanding"* (Proverbs 3:5).

> Never be afraid to trust an unknown future to a known God. —Corrie ten Boom

Complete Faith

The Bible tells us that it is absolutely impossible to please God and to be in right standing with Him without total faith in Him. Why is that? The writer of the book of Hebrews says that it is because those who come to God—those who wish to be in right standing with Him—must believe that He is present in every circumstance and that He will give His very best to those who trust Him completely.

> *But without faith it is impossible to please Him, for he who comes to God must believe that He is, and that He is a rewarder of those who diligently seek Him.*
> (Hebrews 11:6)

Think about it. If you believe that God exists because of the truth you have discovered in His Word, then you are faced with a choice: agree with what His Word says and trust Him fully for all aspects of your life, or reject His Word and refuse to believe.

To put it another way, you have only two choices with God: either you are going to believe in Him, or you are not going to believe in Him. There is no middle ground. It is faith or unbelief. The problem with many people who call themselves Christians today is that they want a middle ground. They want to declare their faith in God but, at the same time, stand on their own merits. They want to trust Him while still having a back-up plan—in case they don't like the answers He provides. But you cannot have it both ways.

God will be pleased with you only if you put your faith in Him. Scripture tells us that there is only one way for you to put your total faith in Him. You must see Him as *"the way, the truth, and the life"* (John 14:6).

Acknowledging Jesus as the Only Way

The message of the gospel of Jesus Christ is familiar to millions of individuals across America and around the world. In fact, according to one researcher, more than 76 percent of Americans (an estimated 159 million people) identify themselves as Christians. If that is the case, then why do so many of us continue to behave in ways that are diametrically opposed to the tenets of the Christian faith, as taught in the Bible?

More than ever in our society, behaviors and activities that are destructive to individuals, families, communities, and cultures seem to dominate people's lives: divorce, homosexuality, pornography, abuse of women and children, abortion, dishonesty on the job, greed, selfishness—the list could go on. All these behaviors and more seem to have people of all ages in chains of bondage that control them, day in and day out.

There can be only one reason why people who call themselves Christians live below the standards to which they are called. Somehow, they have missed a simple truth of the gospel message: Jesus Christ came to set them free and to empower them to live lives of abundance and meaning.

In my role as a pastor and community leader, I find that people are longing to find the answers to their deepest needs. No one *wants* to be in bondage. No one *wants* his marriage to fail and his family to live in turmoil and despair. No one *wants* to be chained to issues that slowly destroy him and those whom he loves. People want to know truth that can set them free. (See John 8:32.) They are looking for real life.

That is the good news of the gospel. Jesus said, *"I am the way, the truth, and the life"* (John 14:6). What did He mean by that? He meant that He alone is the doorway into all the abundance and satisfaction each of us has been created by God to enjoy. As I explained before, God created you and me for relationship with Him, and everything He creates is perfect. The relationship He created for us to enjoy was perfect, with no obstacles blocking the way for us to receive all that He desires to give us.

> **God created you and me for relationship with Him, and everything He creates is perfect.**

Overcoming the Obstacle of Sin

Ever since the disobedience of the first created man and woman, Adam and Eve, our relationship with God has been broken. The Bible calls that disobedience "sin," and, throughout the ages, sin has been the one thing that has kept people from enjoying the good life that God created for them. Sin in each of our lives has imposed an enormous gulf that has kept us from reaching God and being in right relationship with Him.

Throughout history, many people have tried to cross that gulf on their own, through good works and religious traditions, by trying to convince themselves that there is no such gulf, and even by declaring that there is no God to whom we are accountable! But, try as they might, they cannot find release from the bondage of sin or from the deep-down feeling that their lives have gone off track.

The world around you will offer all sorts of methods and systems for living that may seem right at the time, but the Bible tells us that all those ways lead to death and destruction. (See Proverbs 14:12.) The bottom line is this: we can never be good enough to take care of the inherent sin problem in our lives. God's Word tells us that the result of that sin problem is not only separation from God, but also eternal death. *"For the wages of sin is death"* (Romans 6:23).

The blood of Jesus washes away our past and the name
of Jesus opens up our future.　　　—Jesse Duplantis

The Power of Love

If that was how the story ended, we all would be in a tremendous amount of trouble here on earth. If God was only just
and not also compassionate and merciful, then, after humanity ruined the perfection of His creation through disobedience,
rebellion, and sin, He might well have thrown in the towel, left
us to our own devices, and allowed death to cover us in eternal
darkness.

Yet that is not God's character, as we shall see. He is not
only just and completely holy, without any blemish of sin or
wrongdoing, but He is also compassionate, merciful, and not
willing that anyone He created should be destroyed through the
bondage of sin.

The Lord is…not willing that any should perish.
(2 Peter 3:9)

One of the best-known Bible verses in the world, which you
may even have learned as a child in Sunday school, gives us a
great indication of how God turned around all the misery, pain,
and destruction of sin that existed in the world.

*For God so loved the world that He gave His only begot-
ten Son, that whoever believes in Him should not perish
but have everlasting life.*　　　(John 3:16)

In fact, the Bible indicates that God offered this precious
and irreplaceable gift of His Son without any guarantee that
we would receive and accept salvation, noting that God demonstrated His love toward us *"in that while we were still sinners,
Christ died for us"* (Romans 5:8).

The penalty of death was the only way to wipe out the bondage of sin that kept us from the fellowship God intended for us

to have with Him. The death of Jesus—the perfect, sinless Son of God—followed by His incredible and totally victorious resurrection completely took care of the sin problem that separated us from God.

But there is an important step we must take to secure that salvation. According to John 3:16, we must believe. Believing in Jesus is the foundation of all that God has for us in this world and in the life to come. The Bible tells us that He is the only way to find peace and a relationship with God. (See Romans 5:1.) When we confess our sins and put our trust in Jesus, asking Him to cleanse us from all our sin and wrongdoing, the Bible says that *"He is faithful and just to forgive us our sins and to cleanse us from all unrighteousness"* (1 John 1:9). Jesus is faithful to redeem us back to the original purpose for which we were created—fellowship and intimacy with the heavenly Father.

> **Jesus is faithful to redeem us back to the original purpose for which we were created— fellowship and intimacy with the heavenly Father.**

Jesus Himself said that the reason He came to earth was to give each one of us an abundant life. (See John 10:10.) So, when we trust in Him, not only will He make certain that heaven is our home when this life is over, but He also promises that He will pave the way for us to have joy and fulfillment in every corner of this life—in our inner being, in our relationships with others, in our health, and even in our finances. He has a lifelong destiny for each of us that begins the moment we receive Him as Savior and Lord.

Knowing the Importance of Humility and Repentance

While the Bible tells us that Jesus died for our sins and faults to reestablish our relationship with God, there is an important step each of us must take to access this mercy and grace that Christ offers. That step is to practice *humility*. Scripture says, *"God resists the proud, but gives grace to the humble"*

(James 4:6). To be humble is to realize how weak and lowly we are, how helpless we are to change the course of our lives in our own power. That realization is all God is asking for. He wants us to realize and confess our helplessness, our sinfulness, and our complete and utter need for Him. That is called *repentance*, and God will never reject those who come to Him with this kind of attitude.

> The LORD *is near to those who have a broken heart, and saves such as have a contrite spirit.* (Psalm 34:18)

The problem in our world is that humility is not seen as a positive trait but as a weakness that should be avoided at all costs. How often do you hear someone admit that he or she was wrong or made a mistake? When was the last time you heard someone ask for forgiveness? When have you seen someone humble himself before another person, allowing himself to appear weak and submissive to someone else? These days, people are afraid to admit wrong, weakness, or lack in some area. It is much easier on our pride to lie, make excuses, or ignore personal issues that should be faced.

But in God's economy, pride is an obstacle to receiving His mercy, and humility is an essential asset. We must come humbly to God through Jesus, confess our need and lack, and ask Christ to cleanse and receive us. And we must make one more important request of Him: we must ask Jesus to take control of our lives and guide us every step of the way. This is called giving Christ lordship over our lives. It is nothing less than giving Him complete control.

Take the Step

That is the door to relationship with God, the door to being His true child through faith in Jesus Christ. I am surprised by how little emphasis many churches and Christian society in general give to these important steps to peace with God—receiving Christ's cleansing from sin and giving Him lordship over our lives. So many other things seem to be preached from our pulpits nowadays, from social issues to political agendas to self-help systems to an unending stream of theological "hobby horses."

All the while, Jesus calls out to those who have never accepted Him as Savior and Lord, as well as to those who have drifted away from close, warm fellowship with the heavenly Father:

> *Behold, I stand at the door and knock. If anyone hears My voice and opens the door, I will come in to him and dine with him, and he with Me.* (Revelation 3:20)

How will you respond to His call? You may or may not have made that crucial step of faith in Christ. But I can assure you, when you do take such a step and commit all your ways to the Lord, your life will never be the same.

I would like to invite you to take that step with me right now. Wherever you are in life, no matter how bad or good things seem to be, if you will give your life anew to Christ, you will find the safe harbor and future of joy and fulfillment each of us craves. Perhaps you've taken such a step of faith in the past and truly intended to walk uprightly and trust God, but life got in the way. Perhaps you've made choices that you would like to take back. Perhaps you feel as far away from peace with God as you could possibly be.

Wherever you are in life, no matter how bad or good things seem to be, if you will give your life anew to Christ, you will find the safe harbor and future of joy and fulfillment each of us craves.

Would you repeat the following prayer of repentance and acceptance of Christ and join me as a forgiven and accepted child of God? I can assure you that He receives you wherever you are, and He is committed to your success for the rest of your life and for all eternity. The fact that you are reading these pages right now is an answer to prayer and a demonstration that God truly cares about you. Won't you pray the prayer with me?

Jesus, I have heard You knocking on the door of my life, and, right now, I open my life to You. I confess that I am a sinner, and I acknowledge that Your sacrifice on the cross is the only way I can be saved and have a relationship with God. I receive You as my Savior, and I ask You to be my Lord and to take control of my life. Thank You for taking away my sin, for bringing me into God's family, and for helping me to be the person I should be. Amen.

This step you have just taken is so important because it establishes your place in God's kingdom and proclaims your desire to live your life as He purposed you to live. As we will see in the coming chapters, your faith in God through Jesus Christ is absolutely foundational if you are to live successfully and abundantly in every situation.

Chapter Three

God Wants to Give You All Things

In my role as a pastor, one of the duties I most enjoy is helping couples prepare for the lifelong commitment of marriage. It's an important step, one which requires both the prospective husband and wife to forsake all attachments to other people and things that would draw them away from each other and to give their whole beings to each other in love and commitment.

Have you ever taken the time to closely observe a young man and woman in love as they prepare for the all-important step of marriage? For couples in which the man and the woman are truly in love with one another, regardless of what is going on around them, their focus is only on each other; everyone and everything else are side issues. They desire to be together all the time, to find out more and more about each other, and to learn all the details—small and large—of each other's lives.

For his part, the man wants to know about his bride-to-be's likes and dislikes, her favorite color, what her tastes are in jewelry and perfume, and the things that make her laugh, so that he might pull her heart ever closer to his. When they are together, he is constantly attentive to her every need. He opens doors for her, he is especially nice to her family, and he never comes to pick her up without bringing some little token of her worth and value to him.

Similarly, the young woman is preoccupied by thoughts of her beloved, thinking of how she can be more attractive to him and what she can do to keep his thoughts always on her. When the two are together, her eyes always seem to be on him, watching and beckoning, tender toward the one she loves.

But allow me to pose a few startling questions. What do you think would happen to this special, intimate relationship if, instead of lavishing all of her attention and gazes upon her fiancé, the bride-to-be began to allow her eyes and attention to wander to other men, perhaps to an old boyfriend? What would this young man think of his intended bride, whom he had loved, cherished, and dreamed of spending a lifetime with? Do you think they would have a happy and healthy union, filled with trust, hope, and intimacy? Or might the husband's mind be filled with doubt, anxiety, and even jealousy anytime he caught her turning her gaze toward another man or finding fulfillment in someone or something other than himself?

You Are the Bride of Christ

As the bridegroom rejoices over the bride, so shall your God rejoice over you. (Isaiah 62:5)

> **The relationship God desires and promises to those who take the time to know Him far exceeds the mediocre and unfulfilling fare that has become a staple of the American religious experience today.**

The marriage relationship, with all its intimacy and closeness, has always been considered symbolic of the close spiritual intimacy that God created for each one of us to enjoy with Him through His Son, Jesus Christ. The Bible refers to those of us who have made Christ our Savior and Lord as His "bride." This includes men, women, boys, and girls—all who call upon the name of Christ are collectively His bride.

As we discussed in the last chapter, God created us for relationship with Him. But the relationship He desires to enjoy with us on a daily basis is not the casual association that many of us envision when we think about a "personal relationship with Jesus Christ." In fact, the relationship God desires and promises to those who take the time to know Him far exceeds the mediocre and unfulfilling fare that has become a staple of the American religious experience today.

For many of us who have been steeped in the cultural Christianity practiced in America, a relationship with Christ means saying the "Sinner's Prayer" at a gospel crusade or after a particularly poignant church service where our emotions are charged and we feel the need to press in and discover our place in the kingdom of God. For many of us, it is also making sure that we are in church on Sundays, and maybe again sometime during the week. It is the obligation to give of our financial resources—at least 10 percent—and to try (often in vain) to pray on a regular basis while keeping up with a Bible reading schedule.

Sadly, for most individuals today, this kind of relationship becomes an exercise in futility, and, before long, they find themselves throwing in the towel on the assumption that they can ever truly know God or live in the abundance He has promised. They may continue to go through the motions, smiling and praising the Lord with everyone else in church, keeping up the charade that all is well and they are living in victory. But, in truth, their Christian life has become a huge deception.

No wonder so many Christians today have traded in a "fake" relationship with God for the cheap and tawdry things this world has to offer: success, money, high-priced toys, status symbols of luxury, and other worldly distractions that steal their peace and keep them from ever achieving true intimacy with their heavenly Father.

> He who has God and many other things has no more than he who has God alone.   —C. S. Lewis

Resting in His Promises

God does not allow His children to accept less than the best. Remember, He promised us the abundance and wealth of His kingdom: forgiveness of sins, divine health for our bodies, prosperity for our homes and finances, and an absolute over-flow of all His power to help us accomplish everything that He has created us to do.

Across the nation and around the world, countless thousands of good people who love God and are called to His purposes have suddenly found themselves living in circumstances far below what they thought God had promised them. Many have lost homes that they had worked years to purchase and enjoy. Many have lost careers that they had assumed would carry them to retirement. Others cannot find the income to pay their monthly bills. In short, times are tough, and there is no certainty that they will get better in the near future.

What does this mean for God's children, those who call Christ their Savior and Lord? Why are so many of us suffering in ways in which the Bible says we are not supposed to suffer? Where is the abundance that God said was ours, as His children?

I believe that it is where it has always been: firmly secure in God's hand. He has not broken His promise of abundance and provision for you and me. We can take His promise to heart that *"He is good! For His mercy endures forever"* (Psalm 136:1). Furthermore, I am convinced that, despite whatever problems and challenges we are facing in our economy and in society, God will be true to His promise. He will never forsake those He has chosen, nor will He allow their children to go hungry. *"I have never seen the godly abandoned or their children begging for bread"* (Psalm 37:25 NLT).

However, I do believe that God is allowing many of those He loves to be stripped down to the bare minimum in order to re-focus their attention on Him and to help them learn the path to true intimacy with Him. In short, He wants the bride of Christ to act like the bride of Christ—to make their first priority loving and enjoying Him.

Fear Not, Child of God!

If what I described sounds like the place where you are living right now, let me assure you that God has much for you to enjoy as His child. Jesus Himself assures you of this when He declares, *"Do not fear,...for it is your Father's good pleasure to give you the kingdom"* (Luke 12:32). Yes, God actually gets pleasure in doing good to you and your household. He does not enjoy seeing His people suffer financially, physically, relationally, or in any other way. Our suffering in these areas often comes simply from a failure to keep Christ at the center of our lives.

Let's look back for a moment at the children of Israel, whom God chose out of all the earth as His own special people. When God called them, His intent was that they would look only to Him, loving Him and forsaking every other influence and distraction that the world had to offer. He made a covenant of relationship with this special people, promising that He would bless them in every way imaginable. All they had to do was keep their allegiance and love focused on Him alone. Here's what He had to say about His special treasure, Israel:

> *For you are a holy people, who belong to the LORD your God. Of all the people on earth, the LORD your God has chosen you to be his own special treasure.*
> (Deuteronomy 7:6 NLT)

God was saying that this group of people was set apart from every other group of people so that they could be His unique possession, unblemished by all the evil and wickedness that were running rampant throughout the earth. You might think that God chose the children of Israel because they were inherently special—talented or unique in some way that made them stand out from all the other nations. That was not the case at all. When He spoke to them in this verse from Deuteronomy, they were a weak, needy, and pathetic nation. In fact, they had been in the bondage of slavery in Egypt until God led them out under the leadership of His servant Moses.

So, why did God lead them out and call them as His own special people? Moses explained,

> *It was simply that the LORD loves you, and he was keeping the oath he had sworn to your ancestors. That is*

why the LORD *rescued you with such a strong hand from
your slavery and from the oppressive hand of Pharaoh,
king of Egypt.*   (Deuteronomy 7:8 NLT)

If you look carefully at that verse, you'll see two reasons
why God did what He did: love and covenant. He had set His
love upon this people from the very beginning of their existence,
and He had made a *covenant*—a promise—with their forefathers that He would keep them as His own special people, His
treasure. In return, all God asked was for this weak and needy
people to put their faith in Him. He wanted them to trust Him
for all their needs, which He promised to supply. He wanted
them to worship Him alone and not to be sidetracked by the
wickedness that swirled around them through the other people
they came into contact with.

In fact, as we all know, one of the Ten Commandments that
God personally gave to the children of Israel stated, *"You shall
have no other gods before Me"* (Deuteronomy 5:7). He expanded
on this commandment when He warned them that they were
not to make agreements with the other groups of people in the
land that He was giving to them as an inheritance. Instead,
they were to destroy every evil influence that they found in the
land, tearing down all idols and anything else that might draw
them or their families away from loving God with their whole
hearts.

Confessing your sins is no substitute for forsaking
them.   —Anonymous

He Is a God of Mercy

The troubled history of the children of Israel shows how
easy it can be to get pulled away from the important focus of
loving God with our whole hearts and beings. While Israel had
many good leaders who prayed fervently for God's mercy and
grace to cover His wayward children—and who did their best to
lead them—this willful and rebellious nation seemed to follow
every path and listen to every voice that beckoned them, except

for the path and the voice of God. God called them *"a stiff-necked people"* (Exodus 32:9), resistant and unwilling to make the choices that would secure the blessings He had promised.

Yet, God did not forsake them, because one of His main attributes is mercy. He longed for His chosen people, sought after them, and desired relationship and intimacy with them. As with believers in Christ, He also compared Israel to a bride, with Himself as their bridegroom, saying, *"As the bridegroom rejoices over the bride, so shall your God rejoice over you"* (Isaiah 62:5).

Even after Israel's rebellion and unfaithfulness to God had just about ruined them as a nation, reducing them to a shadow of their former greatness, God continued to seek after His children, assuring them that He still loved and desired them. He vowed to reclaim them from their destruction and make them into a beautiful, desirable bride once more.

> *"For your Maker is your husband, the LORD of hosts is His name; and your Redeemer is the Holy One of Israel....With everlasting kindness I will have mercy on you,"* says the LORD, your Redeemer.   (Isaiah 54:5, 8)

Among the attributes of God, although they are equal, mercy shines with even more brilliance than justice.

—Miguel de Cervantes

The Choice Was His, Not Yours

God's desire for relationship and intimacy with the children of Israel mirrors the heart He has for each of us through our faith in Jesus Christ. Just as God delivered Israel out of bondage and slavery in Egypt, bringing them into an inheritance of freedom and destiny, God has also redeemed each one of us from the bondage and slavery of sin. He

Just as with Israel, God did not choose us because of any beauty, goodness, or special attribute we possessed.

did it through the death and resurrection of His Son, Jesus Christ. Just as with Israel, God did not choose us because of any beauty, goodness, or special attribute we possessed. In fact, the Bible makes it clear that, though we were totally lost in sin and deserving of death, Christ still died for us. (See Romans 5:8.)

Today, many Christians are under the mistaken assumption that when they made Jesus Christ their Savior and Lord, it was a matter of their choice. Nothing could be further from the truth. Jesus Himself said,

> *You did not choose Me, but I chose you and appointed you that you should go and bear fruit, and that your fruit should remain, that whatever you ask the Father in My name He may give you.* (John 15:16)

Are you beginning to see the picture? It's all about God's great desire for a relationship with us. He chose us for Himself because He loved us and because of the covenant He made long ago to cleanse us from all wrong and to make us perfect and accepted in His presence, to bring us into His kingdom.

Made in Christ's Image

As I mentioned earlier in this chapter, God created the marriage relationship that husbands and wives enjoy here on earth as a representation of the spiritual truth of our relationship with Christ. Nowhere is that truth more powerfully presented than in the apostle Paul's admonition that husbands must love their wives.

> *Husbands, love your wives, just as Christ also loved the church and gave Himself for her, that He might sanctify and cleanse her with the washing of water by the word, that He might present her to Himself a glorious church, not having spot or wrinkle or any such thing, but that she should be holy and without blemish.*
> (Ephesians 5:25–27)

What a powerful statement, and one that ought to cause each of us to examine the quality and intensity of our love for Christ. Think about it. The Son of God gave of Himself completely, pouring out His life as a sacrifice for our sins and misdeeds, so that we would be sanctified—set apart for His purposes—cleansed, and prepared to be a bride without any blemish whatsoever.

I would like you to take a moment to reflect on your own experience as a Christian—as part of the bride of Christ. Do you feel as though your life has measured up to the standard of being holy and without blemish before God? Do you enjoy the intimacy and close fellowship with God that come from knowing that you have set your heart on loving Him above all else? Or, have other things taken over first place in your life? Have riches, the cares of this world, or other priorities pushed God from the center of your life?

Again, I believe strongly that the tough times many of God's people are facing today are an indication of God's call to them to come back to the simplicity of faith in Christ. Jesus once asked, *"What will it profit a man if he gains the whole world, and loses his own soul?"* (Mark 8:36). You can lose a home, an automobile, a career, or anything else in this world, but that cannot affect your relationship with God or your eternal destiny. Yet God says that putting any of those earthly things before your relationship with Him can put your eternal destiny in jeopardy.

God's love is so great that He will do whatever He needs to do for you to reestablish the proper priorities in your life. God has no problem with His children having big homes, nice cars, or any of the good things of life that He created in the first place. In this life, He wants to *"make you the head and not the tail"* (Deuteronomy 28:13). But His great desire is for all those things to be under His lordship. That is why Christ tells us to *"seek the kingdom of God, and all these things shall be added to you"* (Luke 12:31).

God's priority for you is a relationship with Him, not with the blessings He wants to give you. Otherwise, those blessings will turn into gods in your life—and, as you already know, you can have no other god except Him. If knowing and loving God is your supreme goal in life, if He is your one desire, then all His blessings are yours, and you can boldly declare with King David,

> *O LORD, You are the portion of my inheritance and my cup; You maintain my lot. The lines have fallen to me in pleasant places; yes, I have a good inheritance.*
>
> (Psalm 16:5–6)

Yes, God is your inheritance, and, because of that, the boundaries of His blessings upon your life stretch as far as the eyes of your spirit can see! You have an awesome and unending inheritance!

Chapter Four

Embracing a Lifestyle of Faith

Several years ago, I was on an extended airline flight during which another passenger, who had been flying for nearly twenty-four hours straight, began showing severe effects of flight fatigue. A flight attendant quickly came to the gentleman's aid and provided what comfort and help she could, but it soon became evident that this passenger was in need of proper medical attention. Getting on the intercom system, the flight attendant asked if there was a doctor on board who could provide emergency aid. Before long, a dignified gentleman presented himself to the flight attendant, provided his credentials as a medical doctor, and began to administer the medical aid the passenger needed. This doctor was traveling with his family to a resort for a much-needed vacation. He hadn't boarded the flight as a doctor but as a passenger and a tourist. But the fact remained that he was a fully qualified medical doctor who suddenly found himself thrust into a situation where his knowledge and skills were needed.

Hold Fast Your Profession

Later, as I thought about how that physician had responded to the need at hand, I reflected that this is how God wants His people to respond when faced with the circumstances of life. The author of Hebrews exhorted us, *"Let us hold fast the profession of our faith without wavering; (for he is faithful that promised)"* (Hebrews 10:23 KJV). Some might suggest that what the author of Hebrews meant by the word *"profession"*—or *"confession"* in the *New King James Version*—was merely a verbal declaration of faith. I would suggest that there is more to it than that. In our careers, a "profession" is more than just a job. It is the outward manifestation of our gifts, talents, knowledge, experience, and passion. It is not something we merely "profess" verbally. It incorporates much of who we are.

Likewise, when we come into God's family through faith in Jesus Christ, we are not only given a new life but also a new profession. This is more than simply a verbal testimony. Our profession is a completely new lifestyle. No longer are we to be controlled and swayed by the old emotions of doubt, fear, and unbelief. As God's children, we have become, through the power of His Holy Spirit living within us and overflowing through our lives, "faith-walkers"—people who live by every life-giving word that proceeds from the mouth of God. As such, we are commanded in Scripture to be strong and unflinching in our new profession. The writer of Hebrews admonished us to *"hold fast the profession of our faith without wavering,"* adding, *"he is faithful that promised."* In the *Amplified Bible*, this verse is even more aggressive and emphatic, declaring that we are to *"seize and hold fast"* this new profession we have been given, and to *"retain without wavering the hope we cherish and confess."*

In this day and age of casual faith, too many Christians have allowed themselves to slide into a habit of speaking a faith that is not truly residing in their hearts. Yes, they believe in Jesus, they declare that He is their Savior, and they may even confess and have a degree of belief in God's provision for their needs; but far too many, if their faith were to be challenged through hardship, would be unable to stand and persevere. In other words, while their faith might be a declaration, it has not risen to the level of becoming their profession and lifestyle.

Let me offer an illustration that hits close to home. For many of us, our profession in this world defines who we are and how we function in society. Whether you are a doctor, lawyer, teacher, plumber, electrician, truck driver, beautician, or homemaker, your identity is, in many ways, tied to that profession.

I am a pastor, and no matter where I go, my profession follows me. I cannot get away from it. It defines how I spend my time, how I behave in public, and how others relate to me. Regardless of what people think of me and my message, being a pastor defines what I do during the week, and, in particular, on Sundays. Unlike other people, showing up for church on Sunday is not optional for me; I have to be there. I have been commissioned by God to deliver a message of hope and salvation to those who attend. I must be true to my profession. It calls me to be in the house of the Lord, conducting His business, whenever the doors are open. It calls me to oversee and guide the ministries that issue forth from my congregation and to make sure that what my church and its ministry leaders profess lines up with God's Word and His purposes. I cannot afford to be lax in my duties. Even when I take time off for rest and relaxation, I cannot take time off in my heart and mind from my profession as pastor and servant of God.

Not so long ago, I was with my family on vacation, hanging out on the beach, when a lady walked up to me and said, "You're Bishop Fernandez from television, aren't you?" I had to admit, "Yes, I am." Before long, this precious lady was telling me her awesome testimony and asking me to pray for her. Remember, I was on vacation. I wasn't in "pastor mode." I was in "vacation mode." Still, I wasn't put off or annoyed, and, as much as I might have wanted some privacy at that moment, I took the time, right then and there, to pray with her because I am a pastor; that is my profession.

Years ago, before becoming a pastor, I worked as a flight attendant on a commercial airline. In that profession, we were trained how to react in an emergency when the aircraft was in jeopardy. We were taught what to do to ensure the safety of the passengers. Part of that training was acknowledging that all the crew members, from the pilot to the flight attendants, would be the last ones to exit the plane, only after we had safely evacuated all of the passengers. That was part of our profession. If we weren't able to fulfill that sacrificial duty to the passengers, we had no business being in that profession.

Imagine being in an aircraft over the Atlantic Ocean with three hundred passengers on board. Suddenly, it is determined that the plane must make an emergency landing in the ocean. As soon as the plane lands, you have a chance to get out alive. If you wait until all the passengers are off of the plane, it will be too late, and you will perish. What would you do? As flight attendants, we were trained to put our passengers first. It was our profession, and that was what was required.

Faith begins where man's power ends. —George Müller

Walk by Faith, Not Sight

Whatever your profession, you train for it, you live it, and, if you are going to be successful at it, you cannot shrink back from its requirements. The same is true as a child of God. Your profession is one of faith in God through Jesus Christ. In God's eyes, holding fast to your profession of faith is crucial to your success in life. It is not something He leaves to chance. In fact, the apostle Paul called it a requirement: *"Moreover it is required in stewards that one be found faithful"* (1 Corinthians 4:2).

When you say, "I believe in God," you are claiming a profession that you must walk out in the nitty-gritty reality of daily life. You must walk it out when you are joyful and things are operating smoothly, and you must persevere and walk out that same profession when life is difficult and everything within you screams, *This is too hard! It is more than I can bear!*

Perhaps, like many people today, you are walking through a place of desperation and difficulty right now. In times past, you attended church, sang songs of praise, lifted your hands, declared, "I believe in God," and meant it with all of your heart. But the stakes were not as high as they are right now. Your profession was much easier when you were sure of your next paycheck. The bills were being paid on time. God's faithfulness and provision were tangibly evident in your life.

But now, God is calling you to a whole new level of walking *"by faith, not by sight"* (2 Corinthians 5:7). It is a time when you are going to have to learn to believe and stand for things that may seem impossible. The writer of Hebrews called this kind of high-level faith *"the substance of things hoped for, the evidence of things not seen"* (Hebrews 11:1). Yes, God is calling His people to believe Him, even when everything around them says the opposite. He is calling us to declare that, in every area of need, *"My God shall supply"* (Philippians 4:19).

> **God is calling His people to believe Him, even when everything around them says the opposite.**

If you are facing a deep need right now, you are in a good place—the perfect place for God's provision. I'm not just saying this as one who has not experienced it. I have been there, as have countless thousands of God's people all over the world. And I can declare this to you unequivocally: *God is faithful!*

> I am not moved by what I see. I am not moved by what I feel. I am moved only by what I believe.
>
> —Smith Wigglesworth

Stand Your Ground as a Faith-Walker

Even if those around you are doubting, hold fast to your profession as a faith-walker. Those people need your example and your encouragement. They need you to hold fast. You have moved beyond singing songs and going through the motions—merely looking like a faith-walker. You are the real deal, tried in the fire of affliction, standing fast when doubting would be easier. You are a faith-walker twenty-four hours a day, seven days a week. It's your lifestyle.

Regardless of what is going on around you or how you feel at any given moment, you are a faith-walker and a faith-talker. That is your profession, all the time, and nothing can pull you from that lifestyle. Faith-walkers are not moved by the circumstances around them. And, as a man or woman who has made a profession of faith in Jesus Christ, you have been called by God to be a faith-walker. He does not want you to be moved by the storms of life. He wants you to be moved only by what His Word says.

The enemy is going to try to steal your blessing, your inheritance, and the prophetic word that has been spoken over you about your destiny in God. He is going to try to destroy your marriage, your family, your finances, and your future. Jesus said, *"The thief does not come except to steal, and to kill, and to destroy. I have come that they may have life, and that they may have it more abundantly"* (John 10:10). If you have Jesus, you have life in abundance, to the full, until it overflows. That is what Christ came to give you, and that is what you must decide that you will embrace—nothing less! You must declare, for you and your family, "I will live in the overflow of God's abundance."

That's why you must embrace more than just a casual, wavering faith that's strong today but weak tomorrow. The devil knows how to sniff out that kind of faith and destroy it. That's his specialty: finding individuals who are distracted by the anxieties and cares of the world. If your faith is not rock solid, you will be destroyed by the tremendous outpouring of trials, distress, and wickedness that is coming upon this world. I don't write this to frighten you or demoralize you. I say it to you so you can be prepared. God wants you ready, and He is perfectly willing and able to get you ready through His Holy Spirit and His Word.

Friend, your faith cannot remain static. Your faith must be active. The apostle Peter warned us about our enemy so that we might resist him.

> *Your adversary the devil walks about like a roaring lion, seeking whom he may devour. Resist him, steadfast in the faith, knowing that the same sufferings are experienced by your brotherhood in the world.* (1 Peter 5:8–9)

Two words in that verse tell you all you need to know: *"steadfast"* and *"faith."* The only way to resist the enemy's onslaught of attacks is by standing fast in your faith.

Faith is not a part of your life. It is your life.

—Anonymous

What's Your Profession?

What is your profession? Are you a faith-walker? Are you working for the King of Kings and Lord of Lords, speaking faith, insisting on faith, walking in faith, and calling those things that are not as though they were? (See Romans 4:17.)

Many of you would have to admit that your profession has been far from the faith walk and talk that you know God desires. Yes, when it's been convenient to do so, you've spoken all the right words of victory and abundance, mouthing the phrases of faith. But, too often, in times of stress and trial, you have found yourself speaking fear, doubt, and unbelief.

> **The good news is that God is not condemning you for your wavering. He's calling you to come out and walk more boldly.**

The good news is that God is not condemning you for your wavering. He's calling you to come out and walk more boldly. It's time to grow up and walk in the full stature of a mature, seasoned child of God.

Your ability to walk in faith increases as you practice and exercise your faith. Someone once said that faith is like a muscle. If you do not exercise it, it becomes weak, flabby, and passive. You become the classic ninety-eight-pound weakling, with the devil kicking sand in your face at every turn. But, if you will allow the Lord to lead you through the paces that will increase your faith, you will become a hardened warrior, able to speak to any mountain, any obstacle, and any need, so that in the name of Jesus, what you proclaim will come to pass!

Faith's Starting Place

Faith in God is released in each of us the moment we give our lives over to Jesus. The moment you confess Jesus as Savior and Lord of your life, faith kicks in. Now, initially, that faith may be small. Like the man in the New Testament whose need was so great that he could only cry out to Jesus, *"Lord, I believe;*

help my unbelief!" (Mark 9:24), your faith level may be small and shaky at the start. But make no mistake: faith is there, resident in your heart. That's the starting place for a lifestyle of faith. It doesn't have to start big; it just has to start.

In Romans 12:3, Paul explained that *"God has dealt to each one a measure of faith."* No, we're not all given the same amount of faith, just as we're not all given the same amount of muscle or intelligence. Obviously, I do not have the same amount of muscle as a three-hundred-fifty-pound offensive lineman playing professional football. Nor have I been given the same intelligence quotient as Albert Einstein. In His wisdom, however, God started me out with the proper measure of both muscle and intelligence for the life to which He called me.

The same goes with faith. Some of us are blessed with a larger degree—even a special gifting—to believe God for great things. But rest assured that no matter the measure of faith God has given you, it is all you need to believe God for what He has placed before you in life. And as you use that measure of faith—as God stretches that faith in you through the situations and circumstances of life—it will grow and expand, just like leaven in bread. Thirtyfold, sixtyfold, even a hundredfold, God will increase your faith as you believe Him. (See Mark 4:8, 20.)

Where are you in that process today? Perhaps you have been walking with the Lord for quite a while, attempting to go through the motions, trying to convince yourself and others that vital, active faith is resident within you. Deep in your heart, however, you know there is a problem. It's a problem called unbelief. You see, just as life and death cannot dwell together, just as light can have no communion with darkness, faith cannot coexist with unbelief.

There is an easy way to destroy the unbelief in your life and to replace it with a lifestyle of faith. It is as simple as determining that you will walk daily in the Word of God. The apostle Peter writes that a lifestyle of faith starts with *"the pure milk of the word, that you may grow thereby"* (1 Peter 2:2). Newborn babies need milk, not meat or other solid foods. The need for that type of nourishment comes with maturity.

Many Christians have never grown beyond the spiritual "milk" stage because they have never given themselves to the Word of God. There is no other way to build faith in your life than by feeding on God's Word—daily nourishing your spirit with the truths straight from His heart. The apostle Paul declared that *"faith comes by hearing, and hearing by the word of God"* (Romans 10:17). Likewise, King David explained that in order to jettison the fear, doubt, and unbelief that war against a lifestyle of faith, we must constantly be cleansed by the Word of God: *"How can a young man cleanse his way? By taking heed according to Your word"* (Psalm 119:9).

Many of God's people, regardless of how long they have been walking with Christ, need to humble themselves, realize that they are little more than spiritual babies, and begin to change their lifestyle to one that focuses on God's Word over life's circumstances.

Faith is not merely your holding on to God; it is God holding on to you. He will not let you go!
—E. Stanley Jones

Will Jesus Find Faith?

In Luke 18, Jesus asked a poignant question to which each of us must give earnest heed. It comes at the end of the parable concerning the widow whose persistent request for justice finally brought an answer from an unrighteous judge. Christ offered this parable to contrast the judge's disinterested approach to the widow's need with God's promise to speedily answer when His children call out to Him in their deepest need.

After assuring us of God's quick response to our cries for help, Jesus turned the focus back on us, asking,

Nevertheless, when the Son of Man comes, will He really find faith on the earth?   (Luke 18:8)

This is the question that Jesus is asking you and me. Through His death and resurrection, He has given us everything we need to walk victoriously in this life. We have been assured of forgiveness, adoption into God's family, and abundance for our every need. All we have to do is have faith that God will do for us what He has promised.

Our heavenly Father has always proven Himself faithful in every circumstance. In order for us to live in the full abundance that He has promised, we can do no less than trust Him implicitly, appealing to the promises He has given throughout His Word.

After all that God has done, giving His Son as a sacrifice for your every need and putting in your hands His unchangeable Word, which promises you all things pertaining to life in Him, will you respond to His provision with a simple yet powerful lifestyle of faith? This is, in essence, the question Christ is asking: Will He find faith in you?

Let's take a moment and ask God, through His Son, to complete the work in each of us that will allow us to declare, "Yes, Lord, You will find faith in me":

Father, thank You for the incomparable gift of Your Son and for bringing me into Your household of faith. I ask that You would fill me to overflowing with a faith that can move mountains, a faith that will believe You for the impossible. In the name of Jesus, I pray. Amen.

Chapter Five

Faith in God—Nothing Else!

The esteemed twentieth-century psychologist Erich Fromm once noted, "Whoever insists on safety and security as primary conditions of life cannot have faith."

How that simple statement, coming from a secular observer, nails the condition of a majority of God's people today! As I have monitored the spiritual landscape of our nation throughout my years in ministry, I have become increasingly concerned by the extent to which those who call on the name of Christ have slipped into compromise concerning their faith. In fact, I strongly believe that it has become a crisis in much of the church today. What is most alarming, however, is that the trend toward this condition has been so subtle and gradual that many Christians would not even recognize that they are in the middle of a crisis of faith.

A casual glance at the last several decades in America is enough to see how much many of us have grown conditioned to the assumption that we ought somehow to be immune to the hardships and uncertainties that life throws at us. Many of us have actually come to expect—even demand—a buffer that will insulate and protect us from all risks to our physical, financial, and emotional well-being. Such an expectation has prompted society over the past fifty-plus years to erect an increasing array of social safety nets to ensure that our jobs, our incomes, our health, our retirement years, and our children—the list could go on—are secure from any and all danger.

Every year, insurance companies make untold billions of dollars in profits selling us policies designed to protect our health, homes, financial assets, and just about everything else that we might lose because of natural disasters, illness, or even death. We're in good hands, they assure us.

Over this same time frame, health care has exploded into one of our nation's major industries, with Americans spending multiple billions of dollars on medical treatments, prescriptions, and advice from an army of increasingly specialized physicians and health experts. It has become clear that, to many of us, the health care community has replaced God as our primary line of defense against illness.

> Of all tyrannies, a tyranny sincerely exercised for the good of its victims may be the most oppressive.
> —C. S. Lewis

God Won't Take Second Place

Perhaps the key force that has vied for the allegiance of many individuals over trust in God is the government. Glance at any newspaper, peruse just about any Web site, or watch a few minutes of television, and you are certain to witness government in all its power and glory in news stories, blogs, movies, TV shows, or press conferences. We listen to "experts" discuss at length how our leaders are either succeeding or failing to take care of us, and we speculate on which elected official or political party has the real solution to the problems that afflict our society.

As our nation has struggled with mounting economic crises, to whom have we turned in the expectation that it would solve our problems? As health care and education have felt the bite of a tightening economy, where have we looked for answers? As environmental concerns have taken center stage in the national conscience, to whom do we look for a fix? Government. And, taking their cue, our public officials have been quick to promise us more and more, assuring us that the government will be our protector and caretaker from cradle to grave.

Perhaps the saddest part of this whole picture is that, today, even God's own people do not recognize the great spiritual danger in looking to entities other than the Lord for salvation and security. Now, believe me, I am not promoting the abolition of insurance coverage. I believe physicians and medical experts offer an important service to our communities. And I would be the last to criticize the many social programs—both private and government-sponsored—that have helped individuals, families, and communities survive and thrive.

Yet our insistence upon absolute security has caused us to become a people who have grown used to relying on everything else but God. We give lip service to trusting our heavenly Father, praying vague and generalized prayers for His blessing and protection in times of trouble, and have been conditioned to trust in man, not God. We have made God an option, not our absolute source.

> There are always uncertainties ahead, but there is always one certainty—God's will is good.
>
> —Vernon Paterson

Rest assured, however, that if you are God's child, He will not take second place to anything in your life. The Bible is clear that our God burns with jealousy toward us, and He will not share our love and devotion with another. That does not mean He is small-minded and intolerant. Far from it—His character is defined by mercy and compassion. But because He created us for Himself, and because the enemy of our souls, the devil, works nonstop to destroy our intimacy with Him, there is a choice that each of us must make, and it is a choice that will determine the working out of our faith in this world.

> **The Bible is clear that our God burns with jealousy toward us, and He will not share our love and devotion with another.**

Here is how the apostle James put it:

Don't you realize that friendship with the world makes you an enemy of God?...If you want to be a friend of the world, you make yourself an enemy of God. What do you think the Scriptures mean when they say that the spirit God has placed within us is filled with envy?

(James 4:4–5 NLT)

This short passage perfectly describes the predicament that many well-meaning children of God find themselves in today. While they deeply desire to trust God, the cares of this world war against their faith. But there is good news that we can embrace. James went on to say that God *"gives us even more grace"* (verse 6) to resist the pull of this world and to trust Him. He doesn't put us in this crazy world, demand that we trust in Him, and then stand back and wait for us to fall. Through the power of His Holy Spirit, He strengthens us to stand on His unchanging, rock-solid Word.

The children of Israel in the Old Testament offer a stark example of the tragic consequences when God's people refuse to trust Him. Israel's entire history demonstrates God's faithfulness to them, in spite of their repeated refusal to take Him at His word. In spite of God's love for them—His deliverance, protection, and provision for them in their times of extreme need—over and over again, they rejected Him and, instead, chose temporal, flawed solutions. And they paid a terrible price!

The lack of simple faith led to all-out bondage as they became more and more like the other peoples and nations around them instead of becoming the holy and special people God had intended them to be. Ultimately, they lost their inheritance and spent many years in exile before God, in His faithfulness, led them back to their land.

Tragically, I believe this pattern depicts many of God's people today, people who are looking to everything around them for their hope and security rather than the God who has saved them and promised them abundant provision for their every need. In His mercy, I believe that God is in the process of stripping away many of the things in which we have trusted in the past: money, careers, homes, possessions, status, and worldly esteem. In His mercy and compassion, He is showing that while He wants to bless His people and abundantly supply all their needs, those blessings can

FAITH IN GOD—NOTHING ELSE! ⌒ 65

never take the place of loving and trusting Him absolutely. He will not allow His people to turn His blessings into idols.

Faith is a reasoning trust, a trust which reckons thoughtfully and confidently upon the trustworthiness of God.   —John R. W. Stott

God's Unchanging Law of Faith

God's personal assurance to you of His protection and provision is as unchangeable as the laws He put in place to govern His creation. If you can get this truth deep within your spirit, it will change your life dramatically. King David mastered this secret, and I believe it was the key to His success, as well as one of the reasons he was considered a man after God's own heart. As Psalm 119 expresses,

Forever, O LORD, Your word is settled in heaven. Your faithfulness endures to all generations; You established the earth, and it abides. They continue this day according to Your ordinances.   (verses 89–91)

In other words, when God speaks, that settles it. His Word is eternal and powerful to accomplish His will. We see this in the very first chapter of Genesis, when God spoke all of creation into being. The very words of His mouth are sufficient to create.

Later, after sin had marred His creation and ushered man into the curse of wickedness and evil, we read how God all but destroyed the earth with a great flood. But, even then, God's Word was creative and powerful, and He promised Noah and his descendants that He would never again curse the ground or destroy every living being. (See Genesis 8:21.) With that promise, He made a covenantal declaration, a law that has stood throughout the ages:

While the earth remains, seedtime and harvest, cold and heat, winter and summer, and day and night shall not cease.   (Genesis 8:22)

While we have seen droughts, floods, scorching heat, deadly cold, and other natural disasters throughout the world, can you think of even one instance in which the whole earth has been in danger of destruction? Of course not, because God is always true to His Word. It is the law that governs the universe, and it is unchanging.

Blessings or Curses: The Choice Is Yours

The Word of God, which establishes His faithfulness to you and empowers you to embrace faith in Him, is ever the same. As God declared,

> *My covenant I will not break, nor alter the word that has gone out of My lips.* (Psalm 89:34)

The entirety of God's Word establishes His covenant of mercy and goodness with you and me. Beginning with the deliverance of His people Israel, and culminating with the offer of salvation for every human being through the sacrifice of His Son, God has established an unchangeable law ensuring that whoever will love and obey Him will be the recipient of His mercy, kindness, love, and provision.

By contrast, those who reject His offer of mercy and kindness, or who compromise their faith with the ways of the world, are faced with what the Bible calls a "curse." While that sounds like a strong word, a curse is nothing more than the opposite of God's blessings and abundance, and those who choose to live below total faith in God are already bogged down in a life that is cursed.

Do you find yourself or your family saddled with debt, poverty, depression, doubt, sickness, confusion, or chaos? Do you feel as though you are consistently living below your potential, just getting by and never fully experiencing the joy, peace, and abundance that should be yours as a child of God?

Whether you will live under the curse of lack or soar in God's abundance and blessing is a choice you can make as God's child. Read what God says about those who put their trust in their own efforts, or the efforts of others, rather than God:

Cursed are those who put their trust in mere humans, who rely on human strength and turn their hearts away from the LORD. They are like stunted shrubs in the desert, with no hope for the future. They will live in the barren wilderness, in an uninhabited salty land.

(Jeremiah 17:5–6 NLT)

Now, read what God says about those who put their undying trust in Him. The difference is like night and day.

But blessed are those who trust in the LORD and have made the LORD their hope and confidence. They are like trees planted along a riverbank, with roots that reach deep into the water. Such trees are not bothered by the heat or worried by long months of drought. Their leaves stay green, and they never stop producing fruit.

(verses 7–8 NLT)

God's Promise to You

Whatever your circumstances right now, God's desire is to bless you. That is why He created you: to do good to you, to give your life purpose, and to bring you to such a place of peace and fellowship with Him that the enemy cannot touch you with his destructive schemes.

> **Whatever your circumstances right now, God's desire is to bless you.**

Let me share the testimony of a woman in my congregation who met hardship and despair with an attitude of faith and victory. As you will see, her story is still a work in progress, but it is encouraging to watch someone faithfully persevere, even when the odds are stacked against her.

For many years, I worked with the Waste Management Corporation. I started out as an entry-level accountant and was promoted to Assistant Controller and eventually to the position of Controller, the highest financial position in the company outside of the corporate office. Not only was I their first female manager, I was also one of the few black women in a predominantly white, male environment. My promotions did not come easy. I was passed over many times. Several times, I had to threaten to leave before they agreed to pay me what I was worth. Even with my last promotion, I was paid a subpar salary for my position. Then, following the devastation of Hurricane Irene in 2006, I was asked to run the company's two largest plants. This involved managing and training two office staffs, coordinating two managerial teams, closing the monthly books, and completing the financial reports for both facilities. During this time, several managers received generous bonuses for added duties. My bonus, however, did not reflect any of the adjustments I was forced to make. At that time, I decided to resign and follow a dream of going into business for myself with a former colleague as a partner.

Because I was raised Muslim, my new walk with Christ was teaching me a lot about obedience, prayer, faith, tithing, and favor. I know these principles led me in my tenure at WM. I was earning a six-figure income when I left. In addition to tithing, I was able to give seed offerings to the church each year from my annual bonus checks, as well as helping those with financial needs. God was very good to me.

I invested my last two WM checks into the new business. My partner invested the proceeds from the sale of his home. I know the favor of God was on me because I did not have experience in small business accounting and tax, having spent my career in corporate accounting. My two sons were in college on academic scholarships and grants, so I had very few worries. With a little hard work and God's grace, I was able to tackle the learning curve and grasp what I needed to learn.

With any business, there are good times and hard times. The profits we made were mainly going to cover business expenses and my partner's household bills. He was married with three small children. Eventually, my credit began to suffer as bills went unpaid. Soon, we fell behind in paying the company's debt, which had been obtained in my name. Prior to this business venture, my credit had been great and my monthly obligations were always paid on time, so this was not a good experience for me.

After trying to keep the business going for two years, I realized that there was not enough income being earned to maintain both of our households. I was behind in my mortgage, my car payment, my credit cards, and my student loan. Who in their right mind would have endured this struggle for so long without income to cover their basic needs?

Someone with crazy faith to believe that during the midst of all this strife, something good would come out of it. I stayed focused, believing that God would provide. I refused to dwell on my problems. I slept at night knowing that God would see me through all of this, which He did! Whenever I needed money, it would be there to cover my needs at just the right time. I fully believe that because I was able to give offerings without a bad attitude, God carried me during my times of famine.

After praying and seeking spiritual guidance, I received a message from the Holy Spirit that I needed to start my own business. My partner and his family did not understand the abruptness of my decision, but I knew I had to obey God because He has never let me down.

Two years later, I have a job at the University of Fort Lauderdale and more than two hundred financial clients. My oldest son is entering his first year of medical school at Johns Hopkins University and my youngest son is beginning a career as a computer engineer. However, my house has been in foreclosure since March 2011 and I am renting a car after mine died from mechanical problems. I believe that God is going to give me a car, debt free. I am volunteering my time at church, tithing and giving back where I can because I know I can give my way out of a mountain of debt.

One of my dreams has been to help people, but I never had the financial resources to put myself in a position to compete for those extra clients and financial resources. Recently, I contacted a tax franchise and, after much deliberation, I have decided to work for them. They are financing me for four years in addition to start-up costs. I have been given a new territory to represent. There is no physical building, furniture, or equipment, yet my office is scheduled to open by January 2012.

I'm on cloud nine right now because I feel that I have truly turned the corner. I know the Lord will continue to provide all of my needs according to all His riches and glory. To Him be all the glory. I know that everything is going to work out. I am so grateful for my church and how they pray for me, my contract, my loan modification, my finances, my sons, and my coworkers because I know we all are destined for great things.

If you find yourself living in circumstances that are threatening you with despair and taking your hope, let me offer some words of encouragement. You can turn right now and begin to walk out into a new day of God's glory and abundance. It begins with coming into agreement with God's Word. There is nothing that the enemy of your life would like more than for you to agree with his lies—that you are doomed to a life of despair, lack, and hopelessness. Too often, Christians look at their circumstances and listen to the lies of the devil, who tells them that all they can expect is second best—the hand-me-downs of God's goodness, or worse!

But that is not what the Word of God says. For you, it says something far different, and you have the right—and the authority, in the name of Jesus—to speak in agreement with God's Word over every area of your life. You were created for blessings, not curses.

> *The blessing of the LORD makes one rich, and He adds no*
> *sorrow with it.*   (Proverbs 10:22)

The words of blessing that God speaks over your life and over the lives of your family are the law in your life—a law that you alone have the authority to enforce. That enforcement is called *faith*. Coming into agreement with God's Word is the essence of faith. As you hear, believe, and speak God's Word over your life, faith rises by the power of His Holy Spirit, who resides within you.

Coming into agreement with God's Word is the essence of faith.

Scripture likens God's Word to the rain that He sends out of the sky to water and nourish the crops that the farmer sows in the earth. God sends the rain with a purpose: to make the crops germinate, spring forth from the ground, grow, flourish, and ultimately bring forth an abundant crop that will feed the farmer, his family, and others.

That same growth and abundance are what God says you can expect from His Word:

> *So shall My word be that goes forth from My mouth; it*
> *shall not return to Me void, but it shall accomplish what*

I please, and it shall prosper in the thing for which I sent it.   (Isaiah 55:11)

That promise should fill you with great joy and hope, for God's Word is abounding with the good things He has for you. He declares that as you trust in Him and His Word for you, you will be led forth with great joy and peace, and the very path before you will testify with the same joy of the good things God has planned for you.

Instead of a curse of barrenness and lack in your life, God has promised that the Word He speaks over you will cause a blessing to flourish.

Instead of the thorn shall come up the cypress tree, and instead of the brier shall come up the myrtle tree; and it shall be to the LORD for a name, for an everlasting sign that shall not be cut off.   (Isaiah 55:13)

Are you ready to receive more blessing than you can contain? Instead of the thorns and thistles you may have experienced in the past, you can expect a refreshing harvest of abundance directly from God's hand. Everyone around you will witness God's goodness in your life and will see it as a testimony of what He will do for them if they will trust Him as you have learned to do. Your faith in God, demonstrated before your family, friends, and neighbors, will be a magnet to draw others to faith and relationship with the Father. And what better blessing can you imagine than being a person who draws others into their God-created destinies?

Chapter Six

Fear Not!

You probably remember where you were, what you were doing, and what your immediate reaction was when you heard the news. Most likely, you were watching live television coverage soon after the horrific drama started to unfold.

A huge jet airliner had just crashed into the north tower of the World Trade Center in New York City. A few minutes afterward, millions of people all over the world would watch in stunned horror as a second jet slammed into the south tower. A few minutes later, we heard that a third jet, filled with passengers, had crashed into the Pentagon in Washington, D.C., and yet another had plunged into a farm field in Pennsylvania, killing all on board. Ultimately, we would discover that what we had witnessed on the morning of September 11, 2001, had been nothing less than a well-orchestrated terrorist attack on our nation, an assault that took the lives of almost three thousand individuals.

In the days and weeks following this national tragedy, nearly every American felt an unmistakable sense of vulnerability at the realization that a small group of individuals, with malicious intent in their hearts and minds, had managed to circumvent the security mechanisms of the most powerful nation on earth; commandeer, with apparent ease, four commercial jetliners; and successfully strike at the economic heart of our largest city and our military's command center.

In the aftermath of the assault, many began to ask penetrating questions about the safety and security of our cities, as well as that of our own homes and families. If this kind of attack could be planned and carried out, despite what we had

been assured was a constant vigil of security, couldn't a similar attack—or worse!—be carried out by any one of a number
of well-trained and supplied groups that would enjoy nothing
more than to see America destroyed? If our borders and security were that porous, couldn't someone attack us with a weapon
infinitely worse and thousands of times more deadly than a hi-
jacked jetliner? The imaginations of many Americans ran wild
with fear and anxiety at the possibilities.

Thankfully, as of this writing, in the years since the September 11 attacks, America has yet to suffer an assault of the
magnitude that met us on that fateful summer morning in
2001. Recently, our government was finally able to kill the mas-
termind behind the attacks. And yet, that one horrific event
changed us. It seemed to subtly open the door to a spirit of
anxiety and oppression that has continued to haunt so many
throughout our nation.

The only thing we have to fear is fear itself.
            —President Franklin Delano Roosevelt

A Subtle Transformation

Since its inception, our nation has prided itself on standing
like a rock in the face of national peril and hardship. From our
revolutionary birth in the late 1700s through the tragic years
when North fought South in the Civil War, America's leaders and
citizens alike banded together, sacrificing blood and tears, life
and limb, to ensure that our young nation would stand strong.
From World War I through the great personal and national sacrifice of "The Greatest Generation" in World War II, we were a
country defined by courage under fire. Even through the contro-
versy and upheaval that many of us experienced during the years
of the Vietnam conflict, Americans stepped up to the challenge,
fighting, dying, and giving their best under extreme circumstances. Through it all, courage was the common denominator.

Similarly, when the economic disaster known as the Great
Depression hit our nation in the 1930s, Americans faced financial hardship—along with the cold stares of poverty and

hunger—with dignified resolve and courage, taking to heart President Franklin Delano Roosevelt's words that the only thing we had to fear was fear itself. With limited help from government programs and private charities, families worked, suffered, prayed, and believed together. In time, through willpower, resolve, faith in God, and cooperation with one another, our nation rose above the hardship and pain of the Great Depression and entered an era of prosperity and growth that eventually saw America become the world's economic and social leader.

Business, industry, education, medicine, housing, social programs, and every other corner of our society grew to be second to none. As a nation, we became the head, the leader, and the trendsetter for the rest of the globe. People the world over, from every conceivable background, dreamed of coming to America to start a new life that would bring personal liberties unknown in their birth countries, along with unprecedented opportunities to build a secure future for themselves and their families.

The Danger of Self-Satisfaction

With all of the opportunities, success, prosperity, and abundance with which we were blessed, I believe that a change began to worm its way into America's moral makeup and character, a change that began to subtly erode our courage and resolve to stand together as a unified people. It was a change that made the majority of Americans less willing to sacrifice for the benefit of others and made them reluctant to risk danger, uncertainty, and the loss of their comfortable lifestyles and wealth. In short, we began to grow "fat and satisfied" with our lifestyle of ease and abundance, a lifestyle paid for by the hard work and sacrifice of previous generations of Americans.

A large part of that transformation came, I believe, as the result of a choice many Americans made to put their faith in God second to the pursuit of riches, success, ease, and luxury. With that choice came an assumption that our earthly wisdom was all we needed to solve any problems we would face, as well as to keep us wealthy and satisfied. Instead of making sure to remain humble and thankful to God for all the blessings we enjoyed, too many of us spent our time working, planning, building, and expanding our own little kingdoms, forgetting entirely our citizenship in God's eternal kingdom. Too many of us became like the church of Laodicea, which the apostle John wrote about in the book of Revelation—a group of believers who had grown so self-satisfied with their prosperity and abundance that their attitudes became ones that boasted, *"I am rich. I have everything I want. I don't need a thing!"* (Revelation 3:17 NLT).

Instead of choosing to be "One Nation under God," we adopted an attitude of self-satisfaction and arrogance that opened up America to dangers that, in the past, our humility and faith in God would have protected us from. God is clear in His Word that righteousness—the desire and inclination to line up with what He says is right, true, and good—will keep a nation strong and vibrant, while pride and self-reliance open the door to other sinful and selfish attitudes and actions.

> **God is clear in His Word that righteousness—the desire and inclination to line up with what He says is right, true, and good—will keep a nation strong and vibrant.**

Righteousness exalts a nation, but sin is a reproach to any people. (Proverbs 14:34)

By the beginning of the new millennium, as America continued in an attitude of arrogant confidence in its ability to chart its own course while looking to God less and less, I believe our nation was becoming ever more vulnerable to the kind of attack that we suffered on September 11, 2001. Our thoughts were on ourselves, our prosperity, our future, and our success. Few individuals, even within the Christian community, voiced any concern that our confidence in anything but almighty God might be considered presumptuous.

He who fears being conquered is sure of defeat.
—Napoleon Bonaparte

An Enemy Called Fear

The aftermath of the 9/11 assault on our nation ushered in a tidal wave of fear that seemed to wash over the very psyche of many American citizens. The intense anxiety some individuals felt over the possibility of additional, more devastating terrorist attacks morphed into an overall grip of fear. Almost overnight, the economy began to shrink as manufacturers and business-es struggled to hang on in a marketplace where fewer people were purchasing their goods and services. With the government placing massive security restrictions on air travel, transporta-tion was severely hampered for thousands of businesses, and hundreds of thousands of people were either laid off from their jobs or forced to take pay cuts. Fear of the future caused Amer-ica's economy to slow down dramatically.

Fears over possible nuclear or bioterror attacks on our shopping districts, schools, and other public arenas kept many Americans on edge. In the years that followed, we gradual-ly recovered a modicum of confidence as our public leaders launched an aggressive "War on Terror" overseas. But with the news in late 2008 that many of our most trusted finan-cial institutions, along with several of our chief manufacturing leaders, were either insolvent or teetering on the edge of bank-ruptcy due to corruption and gross mismanagement, America slid into its worst economic downturn since the depths of the Great Depression.

As I write this, government leaders are still struggling to set aright our nation's listing economic ship, even as they assure us that better days are just around the corner. Nonetheless, as uncertainty looms, millions of Americans are being haunted by the growing fear that things are going to get worse in our land before they get better.

While our public officials would like us to believe they have a firm grasp on the challenges that are plaguing our na-tion (and the world as a whole), in reality, the only solution they have put forward so far is throwing billions of dollars at the problem, while political parties snipe and spar over what further courses of action are needed. As of May 2011, our nation's budget deficit for the first five months of the year stood at $830 billion, while our national debt is more than a staggering $14 trillion.

As Europe has experienced a similar economic downturn, rioting and looting mobs have taken to the streets in protest of financial austerity measures needed to keep the governments financially afloat, stoking the fear that, as the social structures that once provided guidance and support, such as churches and schools, are underfunded and on the decline, our own country may soon experience the same kind of violence and anarchy in its streets.

The Only Antidote: A Return to Strong Faith

The vast array of economic, political, and social problems facing our nation, and the world as a whole, are bigger and more severe than any of us can handle individually or as communities. The solutions we have relied on in the past—government, money, ingenuity, and education—are not sufficient to save us. In the end, we have only one option: we must return to a strong faith in God.

For those individuals who have placed their trust in God through Jesus Christ, that is good news, indeed, because He has made it clear throughout His Word that He will never abandon those who know and love Him. Scripture is filled with promises of protection and providence for God's own, regardless of the turmoil that swirls around them.

What I find troubling, however, is that so many Christians today seem to have lost sight of this divine assurance and have bought into the same mind-set of fear that rules the rest of the world. Along with everyone else, many believers seem to be searching for temporal answers and solutions, when they ought to be the ones taking a stand and boldly declaring to their families, friends, and neighbors, "Do not fear! Give your lives to Jesus; put your trust in Him, and He will take care of you. He has promised, and He cannot fail."

It Begins with You!

It is clear that throughout our nation—in our communities, neighborhoods, and families—a return to the strong faith that has always defined America's greatness must begin with those who call themselves Christians. We must lead the way, for if we don't, then who will? In the days to come, as crises in our nation and world become worse, there must be an army of believers standing boldly in full assurance of God's faithfulness who will lead others from fear to faith. In other words, God's people must begin to embrace their heritage of faith and stand against fear in all its forms.

Fear is one of the enemy's chief tools to pull God's people away from strong faith. The Bible tells us that the devil roams through the earth, constantly seeking those whom he can destroy. (See 1 Peter 5:8.) Who do you think it is that Satan finds the easiest to attack? Those who have not been vigilant in building a rock-solid faith in God. The Bible likens those individuals to someone who builds a house on shifting sand. (See Matthew 7:24–27.) When the rain and storms descend, that house falls because its foundation is weak. Likewise, those whose faith is not founded on the unchanging truth of God's Word are bound to fall away when the going gets tough.

> **Your confession of faith in Christ must be based on something solid because, make no mistake about it, the enemy is going to challenge it constantly.**

By contrast, those with faith that is founded on God's unchanging Word—those who refuse to let go of the truth in tough times—are like the person who builds a house on rock. When the storms come, the house stands strong because its foundation is immovable. Likewise, those who build their lives on God's faithfulness will stand through every storm that life can bring.

Your confession of faith in Christ must be based on something solid because, make no mistake about it, the enemy is going to challenge it constantly.

In the book of Revelation, the apostle John called Satan *"the accuser of our brethren, who accused them before our God day and night"* (Revelation 12:10). I don't know about you, but there is no way I could withstand that kind of spiritual onslaught—day-and-night attacks from the devil—without a strong foundation.

Then, John told us how to defend ourselves. Our defense has two parts:

> *And they overcame him by the blood of the Lamb and by the word of their testimony, and they did not love their lives to the death.* (verse 11)

1. The Blood of the Lamb

Being settled in your own heart and mind on the absolute and complete power of the shed blood of Jesus Christ to cleanse you from sin gives you right standing as a child of God, heals all your diseases, protects you from every danger, and provides for your every need—body, soul, and spirit.

2. The Word of Our Testimony

Having God's Word in your heart and on your lips is a ready answer for the attacks the enemy will fling against you.

Contrary to what many believers may think, times of trial and difficulty in life, as well as the attacks of the enemy, will not stop as long as you draw breath. That is why it is crucial for each and every believer to have a foundation of faith that cannot be shaken, regardless of the circumstances or the consequences.

A Personal Testimony

In 1999, The Faith Center, the church I pastor, was carrying one million dollars of debt. I was passionate about the mission of our church: to take the gospel of Jesus Christ around the world. The school we had established, the University of Fort

Lauderdale, was just five years old and demanded a lot of financial resources. As hard as we tried, we simply could not balance our budget. The giving went down, and we were forced to cut the budget, which only made the giving go down again. Finally, we could no longer decrease the budget any further. Believe me, I did everything I could think of to fix the problem, but nothing seemed to work. One day, I threw my hands in the air and said to myself, *Why don't you try what has worked for you all these years—prayer?*

Of course, prayer is what changed everything. The Faith Center's finances and the future of the many families who attended were transformed as we devoted ourselves to seeking God and believing Him for the answer. Our faith rose to a new level.

If the enemy can get you to fear, he can bring distractions in your life that will cause you to think that your situation cannot change. After we began to seek God instead of being distracted by the problem, things began to change in a miraculous way. God empowered us to pay off the entire debt within one year without borrowing any more money. Members who supported our vision gave willingly out of their love for God and their desire to see His work come to pass.

Recognizing Enemy Activity

As financial problems and other challenges have become more common in the lives of individuals and families, it is clear that pressures are mounting on God's children. Yet He is calling us to a walk in which we will hold fast to our confession of His lordship in every aspect of our lives. Like me, you have probably found it very easy to trust God when things are running smoothly, when you can clearly see the road ahead of you. Those are the times when you find yourself declaring with supreme confidence, "I am blessed. I am highly favored of the Lord. I am the righteousness of God and the seed of Abraham. God, I thank You for Your provision and abundance."

But when financial pressures and other problems mount, and there are no answers in the natural, standing firm in the truth requires more than reciting faith declarations. Just because you can make a confession of faith today doesn't ensure that you will stand by that declaration tomorrow. You must realize that the day in, day out walk of faith in God will require that you embrace a real lifestyle of faith—a lifestyle that will stand up against the most difficult circumstances you'll face.

> **The day in, day out walk of faith in God will require that you embrace a real lifestyle of faith—a lifestyle that will stand up against the most difficult circumstances you'll face.**

It is crucial to recognize that the enemy of your soul works overtime to bring distractions that, if you allow them, will negate the effective working of God's Word in your life. Satan realizes that he cannot destroy the Word of God. He knows that it will stand forever. (See, for example, Isaiah 40:8; 1 Peter 1:24–25.) Remember, Satan is the father of lies and a master deceiver, and, for that reason, you simply cannot overcome him in your own power. His expertise is to place obstacles in your path that can knock you off track from believing, confessing, and receiving all that God has for you. That's his "job," and you shouldn't be surprised when it happens.

> *Beloved, do not think it strange concerning the fiery trial which is to try you, as though some strange thing happened to you.* (1 Peter 4:12)

If we are constantly on our guard and remain spiritually vigilant, we will be ready to answer "the accuser." Every day, in many different ways, we are going to face trials and hardships, some of which may test the very limits of our faith. Until now, in America, most of us have been protected from the kinds of trials that believers in other parts of the world have faced. Our jobs and livelihoods have been relatively secure, we've generally been able to pay our bills with relative ease, we've been assured all the necessities of life, and we've faced very little real persecution for our faith.

But what if things have changed? What if we are beginning to see a trend toward trials that will require us to embrace a more aggressive lifestyle of faith? How many of us are prepared to stand successfully and victoriously when our circumstances become difficult, if not impossible, in the natural? If the apostle Peter advises us not to think such trials strange or out of the ordinary, then God must really be calling us to a faith that will hold up under any circumstance.

In Psalms, David tells us that the righteous—you and I—will face many afflictions and trials, but God will be faithful to deliver us. *"Many are the afflictions of the righteous, but the L*ORD *delivers him out of them all"* (Psalm 34:19). Whether your affliction is financial, physical, relational, or in some other area, through Jesus, you can have deliverance. The key, as we discussed in chapter four, is standing on the promises of God. You must hold fast to your profession of faith.

God Desires Mature Faith

Holding fast to your profession means taking an aggressive stance with your faith. Your faith in God and the finished work of Christ cannot be passive. You've got to be constantly making a demand on what you are believing, moving toward your desired aim with steadfast faith, founded on God's Word.

So many people with whom I come in contact through ministry have a double-minded stance toward God. Yes, they love God and want His best in their lives, but what they do not realize is that the only way to get to the place He wants them to be is through the discipline of learning to be truly faithful. Faith cannot coexist with doubt. One or the other will gain prominence within a person's thoughts and attitudes. That is why the apostle James warned us about the double-minded person:

If any of you lacks wisdom, let him ask of God, who gives to all liberally and without reproach, and it will be given to him. But let him ask in faith, with no doubting, for he who doubts is like a wave of the sea driven and tossed by the wind. For let not that man suppose that he will receive anything from the Lord; he is a double-minded man, unstable in all his ways. (James 1:5–8)

Fear and doubt are two of the elements of darkness that God wants to rid His people of in this day and age, replacing them with faith and boldness founded on His unchanging Word. Every man or woman of God, in order to enter into the full stature of spiritual maturity, must come, once and for all, to the place where his or her faith does not waver with changing emotions or circumstances. In order to please God, you must understand this important truth: your faith must define and influence every aspect of your life. It cannot be the other way around.

God desires a relationship with you that is based on your total and absolute trust and faith in Him through the finished work of Christ. He wants your faith to be a full-time profession, one that's more important than anything else in your life. In fact, He loves you so much that if you lack that kind of faith, He can give it to you. He's already given you His Word. And Scripture promises that *"faith comes by hearing, and hearing by the word of God"* (Romans 10:17).

If you lack faith, ask God to give you more. Be like the father who confessed to Jesus, *"Lord, I believe; help my unbelief!"* (Mark 9:24). He will. You cannot live one day with faith in God and the next day with a lack of faith. That is being double-minded, and God makes it clear that those with that kind of an attitude are not positioned to receive what He desires to give them.

If you are wavering and faltering in your faith, His love and care for you remain firm. But He cannot deny His Word, and His Word is clear: advance and abundance in His kingdom are based on faith. That means He will work with you, discipline you, teach you, and train you until you come to that place of faith that pleases Him. That is what a relationship with God is all about.

How would you define your attitude in these troubling days? Have you given in to the spirit of fear that is ruling this world?

Or, have you determined that you will trust in God, come what may? Make no mistake, those around you need an example of faith and courage in the face of darkness and turmoil. You can be that example, if you choose. Let's take a look at the life of an individual who provided that kind of example and what happened because of it: King David.

Chapter Seven

Trusting in the Living God

I never grow tired of reading the exciting stories of the Old Testament's valiant heroes, who faced some of the most impossible situations known to humanity with but one weapon in their arsenal: faith in God. Moses led the people of Israel—a massive group of men, women, children, and livestock—out of the bondage of Egypt with nothing but God's guidance and faith that He would do what He had promised. Moses was followed by Joshua, whose faith in God—learned, no doubt, by observing Moses—empowered him to lead an unproven Israelite army to success against a host of deadly enemies in the Promised Land that God had given them. Through faith in God, the timid Gideon became a *"mighty man of valor"* (Judges 6:12) who defeated the impressive Midianite army with a small band of three hundred soldiers armed with nothing but trumpets and water pitchers! Or, consider Daniel. The faith of this humble man protected him after he was thrown in a pit filled with hungry lions because he had refused to deny his God. Likewise, when Daniel's friends Shadrach, Meshach, and Abednego were thrown into the fiery furnace for refusing to worship the golden image set up by King Nebuchadnezzar, they trusted God to protect them and were delivered unharmed.

These are but a handful of the many inspiring and instructional biblical accounts of men and women who placed their very lives on the line with the certainty that God would deliver them from every scheme of the enemy and bring them to their desired goal. In fact, the apostle Paul counsels us that these Old Testament examples were given specifically for our instruction, that we might be built up in hope and patience by the victorious faith of others.

> *For whatever things were written before were written for our learning, that we through the patience and comfort of the Scriptures might have hope.* (Romans 15:4)

Courage is almost a contradiction in terms. It means a strong desire to live taking the form of readiness to die. —G. K. Chesterton

From Shepherd Boy to Champion of Faith

Perhaps my favorite scriptural example of one who walked in faith and victory is found in the story of David, the humble shepherd boy whom God chose to lead His people, Israel. From his earliest days of faithfully tending his father's flocks of sheep, this young man demonstrated a tenacious assurance of God's goodness and mercy that simply allowed no place for fear or unbelief.

You've probably heard the story of how the youthful David faced the Philistine giant Goliath with nothing more than a sling and five smooth stones. Yes, we know that David demonstrated incredible courage against a formidable foe. But what is often lost in the account is the fact that he performed this unbelievable feat with his faith alone. He had only the assurance that God would deliver the giant Goliath into his hands. No one else stood with him. In fact, everyone else was convinced that he would be summarily killed by this intimidating, foul-mouthed ogre. (See 1 Samuel 17.)

The stark contrast between this young man's undeniable faith and the self-defeating fear displayed by King Saul and the entire army of Israel could not be more dramatic. Remember, Saul had a reputation as a mighty, valiant warrior and had filled the ranks of his army with the strongest and most courageous men that Israel had to offer. They were well-equipped, no doubt; in the natural, they had everything they needed to be victorious on any field of battle.

But they lacked the one key element that would have brought them victory against Goliath and the Philistines: a steadfast faith in God. In fact, as they stood by in fear and allowed Goliath to verbally taunt them, it seemed as if they had all but forgotten that they were God's chosen people. They had allowed the enemy to intimidate them into believing that they were defeated, that theirs was a lost cause.

Into this situation came the youthful David, sent by his father to take provisions to his older brothers, who were serving in Saul's army. No doubt, this young man, whose faith in God had been developed, tested, and tempered against the forces of nature while he tended his father's sheep, expected Israel's army to be larger than life, fearless, and unstoppable. After all, they were representing the God of the universe, whose power and glory were without equal. He was on their side in every battle!

Imagine David's surprise when, instead of fearless heroes, he found a pathetic group of men cowering in fear and dismay as the Philistine giant stood on a hillside across from them and arrogantly shouted, *"I defy the armies of Israel today! Send me a man who will fight me!"* (1 Samuel 17:10 NLT).

David had never been in battle and had never seen a giant as massive and as terrifying as Goliath. In the natural, he, like the valiant soldiers of Israel, should have been terrified. But, as a true child of God, David did not look upon circumstances with natural eyes. No, he saw through the eyes of faith, and, as he witnessed this display of arrogance against God, he looked at the fearful soldiers around him and asked incredulously, *"Who is this pagan Philistine anyway, that he is allowed to defy the armies of the living God?"* (verse 26 NLT).

When he saw that no one else—not even the great King Saul himself—would go out to answer this direct challenge to God's authority, David rose up and declared, *"Don't worry about this Philistine...I'll go fight him!"* (1 Samuel 32 NLT). David's decision was not based on false bravado or a need to impress those around him. No, this was a young man who would be remembered throughout the generations as *"a man after* [God's] *own heart"* (1 Samuel 13:14). His sole motive was to make sure that God's name was honored. When he saw this godless monster speaking arrogantly, David was quick to move into action.

For those who believe, no explanation is necessary; for those who do not, none will suffice.

—Joseph Dunninger

Strengthened and Prepared for Battle

David's attitude in battle with Goliath provides us with a profound lesson on the stance of faith we must take when faced with our own "giants" in life. As we see in David's case, no one had the courage to accompany him as he set his face toward dealing with the enemy who openly defied his God. The most that King Saul could do in the face of danger was make a futile effort to overload the smaller David with his own armor. But David would have none of it. He knew that the equipment and weapons of natural battle would not be sufficient for this fight. Only God Himself could protect, equip, and strengthen him for victory.

> **You cannot read enough books, go to enough seminars, or listen to enough anointed preaching to build up the faith and courage needed to stand for God's victory. That kind of faith can come only by spending time with God on your own.**

Likewise, as you face your own battles against the enemy of your soul, no amount of advice, counsel, and help from others will replace the faith in God you must build up in your own life. You cannot read enough books, go to enough seminars, or listen to enough anointed preaching to build up the faith and courage needed to stand for God's victory. That kind of faith can come only by spending time with God on your own, just as David did as a youth, when he kept sheep in a lonely wilderness. You see, David did not face Goliath until after he had gone through a lengthy period of personal equipping and training by God. He had been discipled and prepared by his heavenly Father in the wilderness place all by himself. During this solitary period of preparation, he was often confronted with dangers, both to himself and to the flock he shepherded. He learned how to trust God and courageously face wolves, lions, and other perilous predators.

Likewise, the testing you are going through right now—be it in your career, relationships, finances, health, or another area—is a distinct opportunity for you to learn how to trust God, face your enemies, and walk out the victory God desires for you. These are His methods of testing and preparing you for the future, when He will give you greater responsibilities and opportunities to trust Him.

Years after facing Goliath, when he was king, David would come back to this theme of preparation, declaring in song that it was God who prepared, equipped, trained, and strengthened him for battle:

> *He teaches my hands to make war, so that my arms can bend a bow of bronze. You have also given me the shield of Your salvation; Your right hand has held me up, Your gentleness has made me great. You enlarged my path under me, so my feet did not slip. I have pursued my enemies and overtaken them; neither did I turn back again till they were destroyed. I have wounded them, so that they could not rise; they have fallen under my feet. For You have armed me with strength for the battle; You have subdued under me those who rose up against me. You have also given me the necks of my enemies, so that I destroyed those who hated me.* (Psalm 18:34–40)

It was God who had shielded David with His hand of salvation, holding him up and making him great through His gentleness and mercy. It was God who made David's path straight and kept his feet from slipping when he faced his foes. It was God who empowered him to pursue his enemies, no matter how big or intimidating they might have seemed, so that he could completely destroy them.

Running Toward the Enemy

David chose to battle the giant with only a slingshot and a handful of stones. By contrast, his seasoned, massive opponent was equipped with the very best in military hardware: a bronze helmet, a coat of mail that weighed *"five thousand shekels of bronze"* (1 Samuel 17:5)—about 125 pounds—bronze leg armor, a javelin, a spear with a shaft the size of *"a weaver's beam"* (verse 7), and a spearhead that weighed *"six hundred shekels"* (verse 7)—about fifteen pounds. His shield was carried by his own personal assistant.

Can you grasp the enormity of the challenge that David was facing and the depth of faith that was required for him to do battle against such an opponent? In human terms, no amount of equipment or weaponry would have been enough for David to match Goliath. And that is the point of this confrontation. David didn't attack Goliath with a sling and a stone. As he sized up his foe, who was already defeated, he made a declaration of faith that resounded throughout the halls of heaven and displayed for all the true weapon of his warfare.

> *You come to me with sword, spear, and javelin, but I come to you in the name of the LORD of Heaven's Armies—the God of the armies of Israel, whom you have defied. Today the LORD will conquer you, and I will kill you and cut off your head. And then I will give the dead bodies of your men to the birds and wild animals, and the whole world will know that there is a God in Israel! And everyone assembled here will know that the LORD rescues his people, but not with sword and spear. This is the LORD's battle, and he will give you to us!*
>
> (1 Samuel 17:45–47 NLT)

God responds to that kind of faith. It is a faith that goes beyond mere dependence to full assurance that what God has promised us, He is fully able to—and *will*—fulfill! The faith that David demonstrated on that field of battle is the same faith that God desires in you and me. He is the same God; He has given us the same promises He gave to David, and He will give us the same victory, too, if we will but trust Him. Like David, in the midst of our most extreme battles and circumstances, we must learn through the Spirit of God that the battle is not ours, but His. To God belongs the victory. When that truth finally takes root within our hearts, we will stop striving and put our full trust in His power. Then, we will see great victories in every area of our lives.

I love the conclusion to this story because it demonstrates this young man's depth of assurance that God was on his side. As Goliath positioned himself and, with presumptuous confidence, made his move to destroy this armorless lad with no apparent means of defending himself, how did David respond? You might assume that he would have approached Goliath with caution, giving him wide berth and looking for the opportunity to get one of his stones past the giant's defenses. But no, this faith-filled young warrior *"ran toward"* (1 Samuel 17:48) Goliath to meet his attacker, placing one stone into his sling. As that one stone left David's hand, it made its way straight and true, crushing Goliath's forehead. (See verses 48–49.)

What do you suppose happened in the camp of the fearful and intimidated Israelite soldiers when they saw Goliath topple to the ground? What happened to these soldiers when they watched this youthful champion cut off Goliath's head with the giant's own sword? It filled them with courage, and they attacked the now-fleeing Philistine army.

> *Now the men of Israel and Judah arose and shouted, and pursued the Philistines as far as the entrance of the valley and to the gates of Ekron. And the wounded of the Philistines fell along the road to Shaaraim, even as far as Gath and Ekron. Then the children of Israel returned from chasing the Philistines, and they plundered their tents.* (1 Samuel 17:52–53)

All of it was predicated on David's own faith in the fact that His God had called him to victory, not defeat.

The beginning of anxiety is the end of faith, and the beginning of true faith is the end of anxiety.

—George Müller

The Battle Is His, Not Yours

The same is true for your daily life. The battle is not yours; it is God's. In fact, for many reading these pages, your circumstances are so overwhelming that you feel you could never overcome them by the natural means at your command. The bills are too great; the relationship is too far gone; the medical prognosis is too grave. The circumstances of your very life seem hopeless. These are the days when God asks those who have called on Jesus Christ as Lord and Savior to fully surrender their situations to Him. God is going to use your circumstances to bring you to the end of yourself—the end of your abilities, your resources, and any hope you have that is not founded on Him.

When the children of Israel were fleeing from Pharaoh after God had delivered them out of bondage in Egypt, that was merely the first step. They may have been free for the first time in years, but they were still being pursued by the heavily armed Egyptian army, which had them trapped against the shores of the Red Sea. God's children had nowhere to go. Their circumstances looked hopeless. But God had led them this far, and there was no way He was going to fail them. Through Moses, God said, *"Do not be afraid. Stand still, and see the salvation of the LORD, which He will accomplish for you today....The LORD will fight for you, and you shall hold your peace"* (Exodus 14:13–14).

Then, God gave Moses some amazing directions. He told the children of Israel *"to go forward"* (verse 15), into the sea! God wanted His children to trust Him so much that they would move through danger and trial. Here is another truth: strong faith comes only through great trials. As the children of Israel discovered, you cannot arrive at the Promised Land of God's destiny for your life without traveling through the dangers and trials that will stretch your faith.

Just as David ran toward Goliath, God directed the children of Israel to move toward the water. He instructed Moses to lift his rod, and, as he did, the waters parted, allowing the fleeing nation to *"go on dry ground through the midst of the sea"* (Exodus 14:16) to the other side, where they were delivered from danger. As their enemies pursued them along that same path, God closed the way of escape. That which had been a deliverance for the children of Israel instantly became a death trap for their enemies.

It's All About Covenant

Fear not, for I am with you; be not dismayed, for I am your God. I will strengthen you, yes, I will help you, I will uphold you with My righteous right hand. (Isaiah 41:10)

God had made a covenant with His people in which He promised to be their God in every way. Moses understood that covenant. David understood that covenant. Likewise, every child of God must understand—and be absolutely committed to—that same covenant in order to live at the level of faith God desires.

> **Many of us may face days, weeks, months, and even years in which we cannot see in the natural how God will sustain us. But sustain us He will, for He has promised to do so.**

Yes, times are tough, and they may get even tougher. The circumstances of our lives may not be easy. Many of us may face days, weeks, months, and even years in which we cannot see in the natural how God will sustain us. But sustain us He will, for He has promised to do so. That which He said to the children of Israel, He says to us: *"Fear not, for I am with you; be not dismayed, for I am your God. I will strengthen you,*

*yes, I will help you, I will uphold you with My righteous right
hand."*

For far too long, many of God's children have equated God's
blessings and presence in their lives with a better job, a higher
salary, a bigger house, or a new car. Let's be clear: God doesn't
have a problem with His children having any of those things,
but material blessings alone do not define God's presence and
blessings for us. True abundance and prosperity can come only
when we learn to surrender to His will and enter into a lifestyle
of absolute trust and holy living.

The Lord deeply desires that we learn contentment and true
godly character, which He calls *"great gain"* (1 Timothy 6:6).
In fact, I will go so far as to say that growing in godly character and being thankful and content with the circumstances in
which God has placed us at any given moment is the true definition of prosperity and abundance.

In this increasingly self-centered culture of ours, many of
us have bought into the attitude that bigger and better should
be our life's goal. But, in God's economy, life is not about getting. In fact, the apostle Paul told his young friend Timothy that
his desire for riches and material success would leave him wide
open to the enemy's snare and most likely lead him into deadly
temptations that would ultimately take him to a godless eternity.

> *But those who desire to be rich fall into temptation and
> a snare, and into many foolish and harmful lusts which
> drown men in destruction and perdition.*
> (1 Timothy 6:9)

What is the solution? Godliness and contentment, because,
as Paul had said to Timothy,

> *We brought nothing into this world, and it is certain we
> can carry nothing out. And having food and clothing,
> with these we shall be content.* (verses 7–8)

God's covenant with you is a covenant of complete, total
provision. Through His Son, Jesus, He has promised that in

your darkest hour of need, *"I will never leave you nor forsake you"* (Hebrews 13:5).

Strength in Weakness

Throughout the Bible, there is a quality common among every man or woman who was used by God: personal weakness. Ironically, it was through those weaknesses that God worked most effectively in their lives. Consider the following examples:

- Even though Abraham and his wife, Sarah, were far beyond child bearing age, God promised this great patriarch of faith that his children's children would be as numerous as the stars in the sky—a promise God is still fulfilling, not only in the natural, but also spiritually, in the millions of individuals who are coming to faith in Christ. (See, for example, Genesis 15:5; 17:4–8.)

- When God called him to lead Israel, Moses pointed out that he was slow of speech (some say he stuttered) and therefore unfit for the task. Nonetheless, God transformed Moses, empowering him to lead the children of Israel out of bondage. (See Exodus 3–4.)

- Through faith, Esther was transformed from a lowly orphan into a Persian queen anointed by God to save her own nation, Judah, from destruction at the hands of an evil manipulator. (See the book of Esther.)

- While we often think of David as a man who had it all together, Scripture reveals a man who struggled with significant shortcomings throughout his life; a man who, at crucial times, was brought face-to-face with his own sinfulness. (See, for example, 2 Samuel 11.) Nonetheless, David's weakness became Holy Spirit-empowered strength when David surrendered in faith to God.

- Even though Peter denied Christ, God empowered him to be one of the early church's chief apostles. (See Matthew 16:17–19.)

- The devoutly religious Saul of Tarsus, who hated Christians and plotted against them, was confronted by Jesus Christ on the road to Damascus. He was empowered for the work of the gospel and became the apostle Paul, who would write almost half the books of the New Testament. (See Acts 9.)

Resting in God's Mercy

We all have weaknesses. But it is only when we acknowledge, once and for all, that it is impossible for us to live successfully in our own strength that we will find ourselves on the road to greatness in God's kingdom. This acknowledgment is key to a victorious life of faith. This is the profound truth the apostle Paul gave us in 2 Corinthians. Like you and me, this confident, highly motivated man had to come to a place of complete surrender before God was able to use him fully. And, like many of us, he was brought to that place through the circumstances of his own life. One circumstance, in particular, Paul referred to as a *"thorn in the flesh"* (2 Corinthians 12:7), and he prayed diligently to be released from it. While we do not know what this thorn was, many of us certainly can relate to the experience of struggling with a personal issue that we feel powerless to overcome.

Can you identify an issue that seems to hamper you in your quest for fulfillment and completeness? Does it seem that the more you fight for freedom, and the more diligently you seek God for release, the more intently that issue keeps you hemmed in and limited? Perhaps it is a financial issue that you have tried to overcome for many years. Maybe it is a tough relationship conflict that never seems to get resolved. Or, maybe it is a physical ailment you have been believing God would heal for years. Perhaps you have even been standing against the negative words and actions of other people as you have stood in faith for God's best in your life. I strongly believe that whatever the "thorn" is in your life, God's reply is the same as it was for Paul: *"My grace is sufficient for you, for My strength is made perfect in weakness"* (2 Corinthians 12:9).

God's desire is for us to come to the end of ourselves—the end of relying on our own strengths and abilities—so that we will finally begin to rely on His strength for every victory. As we witnessed in the case of David, and throughout Scripture, God is able—and eager—to use those who are fully persuaded that, in the words of a children's song, "they are weak, but He is strong."

> **God's desire is for us to come to the end of ourselves—the end of relying on our own strengths and abilities—so that we will finally begin to rely on His strength for every victory.**

Like Paul, we must come to the place where we stop fighting in our own strength and begin to rest in God's mercy. It is at this place that we can let go of all fear in our lives, embrace total faith in God, and, with that great apostle, declare: *"When I am weak, then I am strong"* (2 Corinthians 12:10).

The Weapons of Your Warfare

Let me be clear: this does not mean that you should approach life with a passive "whatever happens" attitude. Just the opposite. For it is only when you come to the end of your own abilities and fears that you will be able to become *"strong in the Lord and in the power of His might"* (Ephesians 6:10). You will be empowered to stand on the authority that God has given you—His Word.

The Bible is clear that, as God's child, you are in a battle against the enemy of your soul, whose only goal is to thwart God's purpose for your life. But it is also clear that if you are vigilant, if you know the lay of the land and the strategy Satan uses in his battle against you, you will be victorious. That strategy, as well as the counterstrategy God has given you for absolute victory, is laid out in Scripture.

A key passage that defines the battle and the weapons you must use for victory is found in the final chapter of Ephesians.

There, the apostle Paul clearly advised us that the battle we wage each day for victory and God's destiny in our lives is not against our circumstances, natural obstacles, or even individuals who oppose us. Instead, he warned us that our daily spiritual battle is against *"evil rulers and authorities of the unseen world, against mighty powers in this dark world, and against evil spirits in the heavenly places"* (Ephesians 6:12 NLT).

That sounds pretty dangerous, doesn't it? Like David in his battle with a giant, we would be in terrible trouble if we relied only on man-made weaponry and methods to confront our enemy. Like David's, our battle is based on our assurance of God's victory. Therefore, the weapons that we raise against the devil cannot be based on fleshly wisdom but must come from God's mighty power, the only thing that will pull down the strongholds the enemy erects against us. (See 2 Corinthians 10:4.) Thankfully, the Bible is equally clear that the only way we can be equipped to wield those weapons and to wear all the spiritual armor that God has supplied for us is by mastering His Word.

In the next chapter, we will discuss how God's Word, hidden in our hearts and spoken with our mouths, will build faith, defeat the devil, and lay the foundation for all the victories God wants to give us in life.

Chapter Eight

Faith and Authority

The great nineteenth-century English evangelist and Christian worker George Müller was often asked how he had developed such great faith in God, which empowered him to preach the gospel and minister to multiple thousands of orphans without ever asking anyone for financial help. His answer: "To learn strong faith is to endure great trials. I have learned my faith by standing firm amid severe testings."

Sadly, much of what American Christians have been taught about faith has not included what George Müller and other great men and women of God learned in the course of their daily lives: that great faith comes only through the heat of testing. If you have accepted Christ as Savior and Lord, then God wants you to grow in your faith and to trust Him to a greater and greater degree each day. And the only way for that to happen is to walk through trials that will strengthen your faith.

The apostle Peter explained that, in God's eyes, true faith in the lives of His children is *"more precious than gold"* (1 Peter 1:7). So often, we seek after material blessings and abundance from God, when, in His kingdom economy, great faith is of far greater value and of more use than material riches. Why is that? It's very simple. We know that God owns all the riches of the universe and distributes them to whomever He chooses. Furthermore, He promises to supply us with everything we need out of that grand storehouse. But, in the scheme of eternity, all of those riches are ultimately of very little value and are woefully limited in what they can accomplish. For example, you cannot purchase God's forgiveness with gold, nor can you buy healing for your body. All the silver in the world is not enough to pay for the salvation of a lost son or daughter. Even if you owned a million acres of the choicest land, it would not be sufficient to heal a broken relationship.

Throughout the ages, men and women have given themselves—body, soul, and spirit—to the pursuit of gaining ever more wealth, all at the jeopardy of their eternal salvation and the salvation of their loved ones. In the end, they leave all their wealth behind and pass into eternity, where the regrets of having made an idol of riches will haunt them forever. Proverbs points out that no matter how firm a hold you might think you have on worldly wealth, ultimately, for all of us, it grows wings and flies away. *"Will you set your eyes on that which is not? For riches certainly make themselves wings; they fly away like an eagle toward heaven"* (Proverbs 23:5).

> **Faith in God will bring loved ones to salvation, heal even the most hopelessly wounded relationships, and accomplish miracles that will shake the earth.**

By contrast, in God's economy, faith is the most valuable commodity, and it lasts forever. In fact, Scripture tells us that *"without faith it is impossible to please* [God]" (Hebrews 11:6). Faith is the very currency of God's kingdom. Faith in the shed blood of Jesus Christ brings forgiveness from our sins and healing for our bodies. Faith in God will bring loved ones to salvation, heal even the most hopelessly wounded relationships, and accomplish miracles that will shake the earth.

Jesus Himself boldly declared, *"Have faith in God"* (Mark 11:22). Then, He explained that with tenacious, not-to-be-denied faith, one could say to a mountain (yes, a physical mountain), *"Be removed and be cast into the sea"* (verse 23), and it would happen. No, it wouldn't be done by a bulldozer, a dump truck, or man's ingenuity but by faith in God. His point was this: when you pray, whatever your need, believe that God will give it to you, and He will—in the name of Jesus. (See verse 24.)

Faith Refined in the Furnace of Affliction

Peter explained that because our faith is so crucial in our lives, it must be refined and perfected. And it is in the furnace of affliction and trials that God does this refining, disciplining, correcting, and perfecting of our faith, until it shines. Recall David's admonition: *"Many are the afflictions of the righteous"* (Psalm 34:19). Yes, it is true that God promises to deliver us from of each and every affliction. But, while we are in that uncomfortable process, God uses those challenges to work within us an ever-increasing measure of faith.

> *Now no chastening seems to be joyful for the present, but painful; nevertheless, afterward it yields the peaceable fruit of righteousness to those who have been trained by it.* (Hebrews 12:11)

While the refining process might bring pain, the writer of Hebrews emphasized that the result will be an increase in the character of Christ in your life and in fruitfulness in all that God has called you to do. In other words, the refining process will bring you a dramatic increase of faith and its results.

You will never grow to full stature as a true believer without going through this process of trials and wilderness testing. Right now, many of God's children are in the middle of such suffering so that their faith and trust will be in God and not in themselves or those around them. Many are facing financial duress to such a degree that they do not know where their next dollar will come from. Perhaps that describes you.

While it may seem impossibly difficult, I truly believe God is teaching His children not to trust in riches or earthly security but in His provision alone. While He has promised us all the abundance of His kingdom, how He delivers that abundance—and in what measure—is all in His hands. We should not be dictating how He ought to bless our lives. He wants us to have the same attitude that caused the apostle Paul to say,

I have learned in whatever state I am, to be content: I know how to be abased, and I know how to abound. Everywhere and in all things I have learned both to be full and to be hungry, both to abound and to suffer need.

(Philippians 4:11–12)

He knew beyond the shadow of a doubt that God would care for him out of the abundance of His riches, and, even when he suffered a temporary setback in his circumstances, he was able to declare confidently, *"I can do all things through Christ who strengthens me"* (verse 13).

"Come See What Our Father in Heaven Will Do"

That kind of bold declaration of faith comes only through trial and testing. You cannot truly learn to trust God unless you are placed in a position that makes His provision—His answer—the only solution to your need. This is the testing ground upon which great men and women of God, such as George Müller and his wife, walked to learn great faith.

Müller himself made believing God for the impossible a lifestyle. Throughout their lives as full-time ministers of God's mercy and compassion to the neediest people in England, Müller and his wife cared for, fed, educated, and raised over ten thousand orphaned children. During those years, they never solicited financial support and never once went into debt, even when, in the construction of five children's homes and in taking care of hundreds of orphans at a time, their needs were great. How did they do it? By making their needs known to God alone and believing Him for the answer!

A story has been retold many times about what happened in the life of Ashley Downs at Müller's orphanage. The children awoke and assembled for breakfast, but there was no food and no money with which to purchase any. A young girl whose father was a friend of Müller's happened to be visiting that morning and witnessed the need. Taking the little girl by the hand,

Müller said, "Come see what our Father in heaven will do for us today."

In the dining room of the orphanage, the tables were set with plates and mugs as the children waited expectantly for their breakfast. Müller prayed simply and with faith, "Dear Father, we thank You for what You are going to give us to eat." There was no doubt in his mind or heart that God would provide *"according to His riches in glory"* (Philippians 4:19).

After he prayed, there was a knock at the door. It was a local baker, who said, "Mr. Müller, I couldn't sleep last night. Somehow I felt you didn't have bread for breakfast, and the Lord wanted me to send you some, so I got up at two o'clock in the morning and baked some fresh bread for you."

Müller thanked the generous baker and thanked God for the answer. Before long, there was a second knock at the door. It was the local milkman, whose cart had broken down in front of the orphanage. "Before this milk spoils, I would like to give it to your children," he explained. He proceeded to unload several gallons of fresh milk for the orphanage.

How had this miracle of provision happened? The simple answer is by faith and prayer. George Müller was no different from you or me in the eyes of God. But, through time spent in the Word, he had come to the conclusion that faith ought to be the norm in the life of a child of God, and he set about disciplining himself to that lifestyle. Müller explained this transformation in his thinking:

> There was a day when I died, utterly died, died to George Müller, his opinions, preferences, tastes and will, died to the world, its approval or censure, died to the approval or blame even of my brethren and friends, and since then I have studied only to show myself approved unto God.[11]

That, my friend, is a place to which every man or woman who truly wants to walk in God's fullness must come: an end of self and a full surrender to God.

God's Miraculous Provision in My Life

In addition to God's Word, personal experience has shown me that God can and will supply all that we need. When my wife, Carol, and I, by faith, moved from New York City to Fort Lauderdale, Florida, one week after our wedding, we didn't have much money. But we knew God had called us, and we were willing to step out in faith.

One Saturday morning, I woke up feeling discouraged because there was no food or money in our apartment. But, as I prayed about the situation, I felt that God wanted me to use my faith, go to the grocery store, and buy our weekly groceries. While my wife was a little skeptical of going to the grocery store with no money, I convinced her to accompany me, and we set off with faith in our hearts and an empty wallet in my pocket. When we got to the supermarket, I pumped up my faith and began to go up and down each aisle, picking out the necessary groceries.

After we selected everything we needed, we approached the cashier to "pay" for the groceries. Carol turned to me and said, "I'll see you outside when you are finished." If there was ever a time I needed my faith to work for me, this was definitely it. With some effort, I convinced her to stay with me and believe God to provide for our need.

After a few minutes, during which we silently prayed and waited, a man stepped through the entrance of the store and walked directly up to me. "Henry," he said, "I was fast asleep this morning when God woke me up and told me you were at this store and that I needed to give you this envelope." He placed an envelope in my hand, turned, and walked out the way he had come in. As you've probably already guessed, that envelope held enough to pay for the groceries we had in our cart, and then some. God worked through two individuals that day. I had the faith that God would provide for our needs. That other man walked in the authority of God's Word, was sensitive to the voice of the Holy Spirit, and was quick to obey. The result was a miracle! Believe me when I tell you, God will get everything you need right into your hands when you exercise faith.

If you wish to know God, you must know His Word; if you wish to perceive His power, you must see how He works by His Word.   —Charles Spurgeon

Approved by God

Surrendering to God means embracing the authority of His Word in our lives. We know that without faith in God, it is impossible to please Him. (See Hebrews 11:6.) The apostle Paul told Timothy, a young minister of the gospel whom he was mentoring, that the chief way he could come up to the standard of absolute faith was to place himself solidly in God's Word every day, studying its promises, hiding its treasure in his heart, so he would be *"approved to God"* (2 Timothy 2:15).

Through Christ's death and resurrection, you stand firm before God in your salvation. Your simple faith in Him justifies you before God.

Let me be clear about one thing: through Christ's death and resurrection, you stand firm before God in your salvation. Your simple faith in Him justifies you before God. Beyond that, however, the Father wants to approve you in a lifestyle of strong faith that will cover every area of your life. And that approval can come only through time spent in His Word.

Your word I have hidden in my heart, that I might not sin against You!   (Psalm 119:11)

In order to stay in that place where his words, thoughts, and actions were pleasing to God, King David had to hide God's Word in his heart. That meant he spent time throughout the day reading, thinking about, and talking to God about His holy Word. David knew from a lifetime of experience that without God's Word saturating his heart and mind, he had a tendency to slip into thoughts, attitudes, actions, and habits that were destructive to him and to those around him. (See David's infatuation with Bathsheba in 2 Samuel 11.) When he kept God's

Word foremost in his life, however, he was protected from sin, disobedience, and unbelief.

Likewise, you and I will find our foundation for faith and victory only in God's Word. In fact, the apostle Paul confirmed that strong, vital faith—the kind that will stand firm in the most extreme circumstances of life—comes by being constantly immersed in God's Word.

> *Faith comes by hearing, and hearing by the word of God.* (Romans 10:17)

It is only in God's Word that we will discover the foundation for the authority we have as believers. Your success in this life, as a child of God, hinges on your knowing who you are in Christ, and who Christ is in you. The Bible says that Christ in you is your *"hope of glory"* (Colossians 1:27)—that is, the only hope you have for experiencing God's blessings and abundance in life.

By His Word, God has promised to give us wisdom and revelation of what our relationship with Him is all about so that we can stand fully in the hope of His calling and receive the complete riches of His inheritance. His Word will give us a revelation of the great power and authority that are in us through Jesus Christ.

> *That you may know what is the hope of His calling, what are the riches of the glory of His inheritance in the saints, and what is the exceeding greatness of His power toward us who believe, according to the working of His mighty power.* (Ephesians 1:18–19)

As believers, we find our power and authority in God's Word alone.

The writer of Hebrews explained that God's Word working in your life *"is living and powerful, and sharper than any two-edged sword, piercing even to the division of soul and spirit, and of joints and marrow, and is a discerner of the thoughts and intents of the heart"* (Hebrews 4:12). When you place yourself under the authority of God's Word, it will become the authority by which you walk in this world. It will define how you face issues that, in the past, have caused you to flounder in defeat. It will cause you to see with spiritual eyes and empower you by the Holy Spirit to live victoriously on every level. It will change the way you think, the way you talk, and the way you respond to circumstances in life. Most important, walking in the authority of God's Word will make you fruitful in God's kingdom, empowering you to do God's will and to fulfill His destiny for your life.

It's All About Authority

The problem with so many of God's people today is that they have not learned to walk in the authority of God's Word. Instead, in times of difficulty or stress, when faith is essential, they find themselves leaning on their own understanding and reasoning rather than on God's Word. Their circumstances, good or bad, become the barometer of their faith. If things are going well, their confession is confident: "I am blessed, and God is my provider." But if circumstances begin to challenge them, if trials and frustrations become too great, their faith begins to flag, and their words turn to doubt, despair, and unbelief. They become like the double-minded person the apostle James wrote about, who was wanting to believe in God but still retaining doubts in his mind. (See James 1:8.) Half-baked faith will get you nowhere. You must be willing and ready to stand in stalwart faith in God's Word, speaking it authoritatively over every situation in life, not being swayed by circumstances. That is the only way to see the fruit of faith in your life.

Jesus said,

> *If you have faith and do not doubt,…if you say to this mountain, "Be removed and be cast into the sea," it will be done. And whatever things you ask in prayer, believing, you will receive.* (Matthew 21:21–22)

He was not talking about easy faith and casual prayer. He was talking about the kind of faith that perseveres when everything says the situation is impossible. He was talking about faith that will not take no for an answer, the kind of faith that declares God's Word of promise in the face of every opposing circumstance and power. Jesus was talking to those individuals who have been tried in the fire of affliction and have come to such a place of surrender that the Word of God is the absolute authority in their lives.

Does that describe you, or someone you would like to be? God knows our weaknesses and strengths, and He realizes that many of His children are not at a place where they are walking in the absolute authority of His Word. Rest assured, however, He also will not reject those who come to Him, saying, *"Lord, I believe; help my unbelief"* (Mark 9:24). He desires that we all come to the full stature for which we were created—the place where our words line up with His Word.

"Out of the same mouth proceed blessing and cursing" (James 3:10). Not only will our words impact those around us, either negatively or positively, but they also have the power to impact our own lives. How often do you find yourself complaining about something in your life, or speaking negatively about some situation you are going through? How often have you allowed your words to run counter to what it says in God's Word? This cannot be the case for the child of God. Just as a flowing fountain of cold spring water cannot also spew forth a stream of brackish, bitter salt water, God's people cannot speak life and death at the same time. (See verses 11–12.)

> **Just as a flowing fountain of cold spring water cannot also spew forth a stream of brackish, bitter salt water, God's people cannot speak life and death at the same time.**

If that sounds familiar, you are not alone. We have all "been there, done that." But we do not have to stay in that place of unbelief and doubt, allowing our words to curse our future and destiny.

David was a person much like you and me. He was subject to the same temptations and, at times, struggled with believing God. That is why He vowed,

> *Let the words of my mouth and the meditation of my heart be acceptable in Your sight, O LORD, my strength and my Redeemer.* (Psalm 19:14)

David acknowledged the fact that God was His strength and Redeemer. He understood that everything he was and everything he had were because of God's mercy and compassion over his life. Yet David also understood that he was inclined to forget those blessings of God, and that, in those times, he would begin to speak words of fear and unbelief. So, he sought the Lord in order to make his words and thoughts, once again, line up with God's Word. He knew that in order to walk in the fullness of God's provision, he had to walk in agreement with God. David's words had to align with a declaration of faith.

The Power of Agreement

In order for us to be fully pleasing to God, the thoughts of our hearts and the words that we speak must be acceptable— that is, they must be in agreement with His Word.

> *Death and life are in the power of the tongue, and those who love it will eat its fruit.* (Proverbs 18:21)

The writer of Proverbs knew that, ultimately, we are destined to reap that which we sow with our mouths. Our God is a God of life, and His desire is that, in the same way that He used His words to create life and abundance (see Genesis 1), so, too, we will speak out life and abundance as our mouths are filled with His Word.

> *This Book of the Law shall not depart from your mouth, but you shall meditate in it day and night, that you may observe to do according to all that is written in it. For then you will make your way prosperous, and then you will have good success.* (Joshua 1:8)

When God led the children of Israel into the Promised Land, He told their leader, Joshua, that His Word was to be constantly in their thoughts and in their speech so that they could be certain of obeying all that He had commanded them to do. Obeying God is essential in order to reap His blessings. In fact, the only way we can know His will for our lives—for our attitudes, for our speech, and for our conduct—is by knowing His Word and being reminded of it constantly.

That is why it is important for you personally to be in God's Word every day, reading it, meditating on its meaning and impact in your life, and declaring it over yourself, your family, and your circumstances. When you discipline yourself to speak the Word of God, agreeing with its power and truth, it will become a part of your thoughts, your attitudes, and your speech. And it will change your life.

There is a quote that says,

Watch your thoughts, for they become words.
Watch your words, for they become actions.
Watch your actions, for they become habits.
Watch your habits, for they become character.
Watch your character, for it becomes your destiny.

—Unknown

There is a progression in your life that begins with what is in your heart and mind. Are you filling your mind with hours of television, secular music and movies, Internet filth, and so forth? If so, that is what you will eventually come into agreement with. It will fill your thoughts, come out through your words, influence your actions, and ultimately define your character and destiny.

Jesus said, *"Out of the abundance of the heart the mouth speaks"* (Matthew 12:34). Your tongue has the power to speak both life and death. If you fill your heart with things that put you in bondage—things that are destructive—that is what you can expect to get back in return. By contrast, if you fill your mind with the powerful, life-giving Word of God, then your mind, your heart, and your words will come into agreement with the God of life! Your mouth will become a wellspring of His blessings, both for yourself and for others.

God's Word is a creative power, and it is impossible for it to be unfruitful.

> *So shall My word be that goes forth from My mouth; it shall not return to Me void, but it shall accomplish what I please, and it shall prosper in the thing for which I sent it.* (Isaiah 55:11)

When God's Word goes forth, it will always accomplish the purpose for which He sent it. It will always prosper! So, if the Word of God is at work in your heart and in your conversation, you can be certain that your life will be in agreement with God—and that you will prosper!

> **When God's Word goes forth, it will always accomplish the purpose for which He sent it.**

Putting It into Practice

In this day and age, with so many people facing hardships and trials, God does not intend for you to walk without protection or without the proper weapons to wage warfare against the enemy. He wants you to have *"the sword of the Spirit, which is the word of God"* (Ephesians 6:17), working actively and powerfully in your life. You may ask, "I'd like that, too, but how do I start?" The answer is simple: begin filling your heart and your mind with God's Word and speaking it over key areas in your life.

A very practical way to start is by gathering key Scripture passages that speak to where you are. Turn them into powerful declarations that will change your life. For example:

God's Word declares:

> *For* [God] *made* [Jesus Christ] *who knew no sin to be sin for us, that we might become the righteousness of God in Him.* (2 Corinthians 5:21)

You declare:

"I am the righteousness of God in Christ Jesus."

God's Word declares:

If anyone is in Christ, he is a new creation; old things have passed away; behold, all things have become new.
(2 Corinthians 5:17)

You declare:

"I am in Christ; therefore, I am a new creation, a new person. All the old, destructive patterns of my past life are gone. God has filled my life with new thoughts, new motives, new actions, new words, and new blessings of abundance!"

God's Word declares:

"No weapon formed against you shall prosper, and every tongue which rises against you in judgment You shall condemn. This is the heritage of the servants of the Lord, *and their righteousness is from Me," says the* Lord.
(Isaiah 54:17)

You declare:

"No weapon that the devil—or anyone on earth—uses to try to hurt or hinder me will prosper. Every word that is raised against me in judgment, I curse and reject, in the name of Jesus. I am a servant of God, and I stand fully justified in my position in the righteousness of Christ Jesus."

God's Word declares:

My God shall supply all your need according to His riches in glory by Christ Jesus. (Philippians 4:19)

You declare:

"God will supply every need I have—physical, spiritual, financial, or anything else—out of His abundant storehouse. I will not be afraid of lack, because He has promised to be my supply, in the name of Jesus."

These are just four short but powerful Scripture passages. God's Word is filled with an infinite supply of truth and power for your every need. All you have to do is access His Word in your life. He has promised that it will not return void but will accomplish that purpose for which He has sent it forth—blessings and fullness for your life.

His heart is filled with love and mercy for you, as evidenced by the sacrifice of His Son at Calvary. Through that perfect gift of salvation, you have entered into a fellowship with the Father that gives you the absolute authority to speak His Word and to see results in your circumstances.

God is faithful. He cannot go back on His Word of promise for you. Believe it and receive it!

Part II:

FAMILY

In every conceivable manner, the family is a link to our past, a bridge to our future.

—Alex Haley
Author, *Roots*

The family you come from isn't as important as the family you're going to have.

—Ring Lardner
Journalist and screenwriter

You don't choose your family. They are God's gift to you, as you are to them.

—Archbishop Desmond Tutu
Nobel Peace prize recipient and Anglican Archbishop

Chapter Nine

There's a Famine in the Land

On the morning of January 23, 1996, Joe Wright, senior pastor of Central Christian Church in Wichita, Kansas, stood before the members of the Kansas House of Representatives to offer a prayer of blessing that was written by Bob Russell, pastor of Southeast Christian Church, in Louisville, Kentucky. It was to provide spiritual guidance as the state's lawmakers began a new legislative session. What the assembled elected officials expected, I suspect, was a vague and generalized prayer, offered to an unidentified and unspecific God—a prayer filled with inoffensive, safe, "politically correct" rhetoric. What the bipartisan collection of lawmakers heard instead was one humble man's heartfelt call to national repentance, a no-nonsense appeal for God's mercy on a nation and people who had lost their way.

Not surprisingly, Wright's simple entreaty, made without guile or political party bias, filled a segment of the lawmakers with rage at his "intolerance" and "insensitivity" toward the many individuals and groups whose conduct and lifestyles were exposed as sinful through his prayer. The fact that this pastor's intercession became national and international news—and is, to this day, recited by laymen and clergy alike, due to how effectively it defined our nation's continuing spiritual deterioration—is a powerful demonstration that millions of Americans embrace the spirit of repentance that empowered his prayer. Below, word for word, is Bob Russell's prayer, as read by Pastor Wright that morning:

> Heavenly Father, we come before You today to ask Your
> forgiveness and seek Your direction and guidance.

We know Your Word says, *"Woe to those who call evil good"* (Isaiah 5:20), but that's exactly what we've done.

We have lost our spiritual equilibrium and inverted our values.

We confess that...

We have ridiculed the absolute truth of Your Word and called it moral pluralism.

We have worshipped other gods and called it multiculturalism.

We have endorsed perversion and called it an alternative lifestyle.

We have exploited the poor and called it the lottery.

We have neglected the needy and called it self-preservation.

We have rewarded laziness and called it welfare.

We have killed our unborn and called it choice.

We have shot abortionists and called it justifiable.

We have neglected to discipline our children and called it building esteem.

We have abused power and called it political savvy.

We have coveted our neighbors' possessions and called it ambition.

We have polluted the air with profanity and pornography and called it freedom of expression.

We have ridiculed the time-honored values of our forefathers and called it enlightenment.

Search us, O God, and know our hearts today; try us and see if there be some wicked way in us; cleanse us from every sin and set us free.

Guide and bless these men and women who have been sent here by the people of Kansas, and who have been ordained by You to govern this great state.

Grant them Your wisdom to rule and may their decisions direct us to the center of Your will. I ask it in
the name of Your Son, the living Savior, Jesus Christ.
Amen.[12]

Once Upon a Time in America

Believe it or not, there was a time in our nation when the
moral compass and spiritual fortitude displayed by Pastor
Wright were the rule, not the exception, for Christian leaders.
In fact, for most of this nation's history, pastors and priests
were considered important leaders, both locally and nationally.
They took it as their divinely commissioned duty to speak out
from their pulpits, from public squares, through newspapers, or
wherever else opportunity arose, preaching and providing godly
counsel on moral and spiritual issues that impacted America,
its communities, and its people.

Consider, for example, the men and women in the mid-
1800s who took the lead in speaking out against slavery, an
unspeakable practice that ran in direct opposition to the Declaration of Independence's assertion that "all men are created
equal, that they are endowed by their Creator with certain un-
alienable rights."

There was a time in America when such pressing national
issues such as those that are now working to destroy our society—legalized abortion, homosexual behavior, and the prohi-
bition of prayer in public schools—would have brought swift,
righteous condemnation from nearly every corner of America's
Christian community.

Not so today. While a small core of concerned individuals
and groups are speaking out clearly for a return to America's
godly heritage, by and large, Christian leaders today have focused their attention almost exclusively on what happens within the walls of their own church buildings. Church programs
and agendas are often designed exclusively to increase the
numbers of individuals sitting in the pews on a Sunday and to
keep families engaged in congregational life, while little effort is

given to the more important goal of engaging their hearts in the pursuit of knowing God and living holy lives.

Worse yet, some of America's most storied denominations—many of which helped to lead the way in America's stand as a pious, God-fearing nation—have now almost completely abandoned God's Word as their final authority, boldly placing their stamp of approval on behaviors condemned in Scripture.

Consider, for example, that in August 2009, the Evangelical Lutheran Church in America (ELCA)—the country's largest Lutheran denomination, with some 4.8 million members—voted to allow non-celibate homosexual men and women to become ordained ministers in their congregations. Many observers thought it was more than mere coincidence that on the very day of the vote, a tornado struck the downtown Minneapolis convention center where the vote was taking place, severely damaging a cross on the steeple of a church located on the same street.

Other once respected Christian denominations have followed the same path, not only disregarding Scripture's condemnation of such behavior but also celebrating sin and immorality in the church and even teaching children and young people that such behavior is acceptable.

If the foundations are destroyed, what can the righteous do? (Psalm 11:3)

Foundations Under Assault

It is not just the realm of behavior and overt sinfulness that has undermined Christian faith in America. The very foundations of what it means to be a Christian seem to be under attack. One of the most blatant examples of this occurred in the summer of 2009, when the presiding bishop of a mainline American denomination labeled as "heresy" the clearly scriptural tenet that "we can be saved as individuals, that any of us alone can be in right relationship with God."[13] The bishop also appeared to denigrate the notion that personal words of repentance and acceptance of Christ as Savior and Lord can save an individual, labeling such a prayer a "verbal formula" that amounts to "a form of idolatry."[14]

Such a statement from a supposed servant of God—a person called to offer counsel and direction to spiritually searching people—is simply unacceptable. To an ever greater degree, individuals and families are being taught errors and lies when they need truth and a solid foundation for life and eternity. The Bible is clear that our words, spoken individually, are crucial to our salvation.

> *If you confess with your mouth the Lord Jesus and believe in your heart that God has raised Him from the dead, you will be saved.*   (Romans 10:9)

In this verse, the apostle Paul plainly stated that if we, as individuals, make a personal confession of Christ's lordship in our lives and believe in our hearts the truths of the gospel, we, as individuals, will be saved. Scripture is clear that Jesus Christ came and died to save sinful people on an individual basis. Offering people anything other than the hope of the gospel of Jesus Christ is a recipe for disaster in our hearts, in our homes, and in our nation.

> A holy life will produce the deepest impression. Just like lighthouses blow no horns; they just shine.
> —D. L. Moody

Too Much like the World

Christian researcher George Barna has spent years monitoring the moral and spiritual condition of America. In a compelling study, he observed with alarm that, increasingly, those who consider themselves Christians are behaving more and more like the world, adopting its attitudes, its styles, and its actions. While we are called to be salt and light (see Matthew 5:13–16), influencing those around us with the life-transforming love and authority of God, too many believers are being overcome by the darkness of the world and find themselves in bondage to life-styles they should be free from. Barna noted that, lacking the "loving, authoritative, healing, and compelling influence"[15] that previous generations found in churches based on the truths of God's Word, Americans are, by and large, "piecing together a customized version of faith"[16] that fits their worldview. And such a move is wreaking havoc on our homes, our communities, and our nation as a whole.

While faith used to be founded solidly on God's Word and the traditions of a Bible-based church, the faith embraced by many individuals today puts self at the center. "We have demystified God, befriended Jesus, abandoned the Holy Spirit, and forgiven and even warmed up to Satan," observed Barna. "Few Americans possess a sense of awe, fear, or trembling related to God."[17]

In an address to the Evangelical Press Association in 2009, Barna said,

> Few Americans possess a sense of awe, fear, or trembling related to God. Just think about the shift in mottos that characterize our nation. We talked about one nation under God, but today really we are one nation under self, sometimes aided by one or more gods. We shifted from a nation that said "In God We Trust" to "Reality and self we trust." We transitioned from being a land of the free and the home of the brave, to now we are the land of the indebted and the home of the self-indulgent. We also shifted from a land that believes you can be all you can be to now it's get all you can get.[18]

Families Turning from the Source of Truth

While many factors may have contributed to this grave deterioration of the values that once made America strong, I believe that perhaps the most crucial has been a consistent turning from an active, emphatic attention to God's Word in our churches and a subsequent turning away from God in our homes and families.

Consider that, for the past twenty years, there has been a gradual exodus of Americans from church. Statistics show that overall church attendance in America has dropped from 49 percent in 1991 to only 40 percent in 2011—meaning that nearly one in five people stopped attending church during that time. In 1991, 24 percent of American adults were unchurched. Today, that figure has risen to 37 percent—an increase of more than 50 percent.[19]

Studies by the Barna Group have broken down this exodus by generation. For "Elders"—those born between 1927 and 1945—the percentage of unchurched has risen from 21 percent in 1991 to 29 percent in 2011. For "Baby Boomers"—born 1946 to 1964—the news is even worse. Their church attendance dropped by 12 percent during the same period. The percentage of unchurched Baby Boomers has gone from 23 percent in 1991 to 41 percent in 2011, making them the most unlikely of the generations studied to attend church. Unchurched "Baby Busters"—born 1965 to 1983—rose from 31 percent in 1991 to 39 percent.[20]

And, although "Millennials"—born 1984 or after—were only children in 1991, a study by the Pew Forum holds little hope for the future, showing that only 18 percent of these young people report weekly attendance at religious services of any kind.[21]

Such statistics demonstrate that a majority of Americans have come to believe that what happens inside the average church has little relevance to their lives. In many cases, they could be right. After all, if denominations that once preached the Word of God from their pulpits now make decisions that conflict with what is in its pages—and even question whether or not it is divinely inspired—is it any wonder that the average American would conclude that the church has nothing important to offer?

The result of this mass exodus from many of today's "irrelevant" churches is individuals and families who are spiritually rudderless in an increasingly confusing world that declares, "There are no absolutes! Believe whatever you want and do whatever feels right!"

We are starving for God's Word. But there is a way back to becoming a strong nation once again—a nation with godly individuals, families, and communities.

At Odds with God's Plan

Like America, a country that has been blessed by God in so many ways, the ancient nation of Israel was on the receiving end of God's great favor. In fact, Israel had been chosen by God to be a special people, one that would show forth His mercy and goodness to all the nations of the world. They had been raised up by God to know Him, to follow His ways, and to live above the evil and wickedness in which the rest of the world had been walking. God told Israel that they were to be holy—that is, to be above sin and wrongdoing in every way—because that was His character, and they were His chosen people.

> *You must be holy because I, the LORD, am holy. I have set you apart from all other people to be my very own.*
> (Leviticus 20:26 NLT)

Unfortunately, the history of Israel is one of often being at odds with God's ways. In fact, throughout much of the Old Testament, the children of Israel, like many Christians today, allowed the sin and wickedness of people around them to influence their own attitudes and behavior. Instead of worshipping God alone, many of them began worshipping idols and embracing strange religious customs.

In His mercy, God had patience with them, sending prophets and messengers to warn them of the consequences of their sin. His message was this: "Repent of your sinful ways. Come back to My ways. Follow Me, and I will continue to bless you. If you don't, you will face My strong discipline, a discipline that will remove all the blessings I have given you, so that, in your misery and suffering, you will come back to Me—and I will heal you."

God sent His people a humble messenger by the name of Amos. This lowly farmer and shepherd was commissioned by

God for a specific purpose: to warn the nation of Israel to repent of their pride and comfortable lifestyles, which had caused them to turn from God.

When God had first positioned Israel to be His people, He had told them that all the wonderful blessings He was going to bestow upon them—lands, houses, food, and wealth—would have the potential of making them lazy and complacent.

> *But that is the time to be careful! Beware that in your plenty you do not forget the* Lord *your God and disobey his commands, regulations, and decrees that I am giving you today. For when you have become full and prosperous and have built fine homes to live in, and when your flocks and herds have become very large and your silver and gold have multiplied along with everything else, be careful! Do not become proud at that time and forget the* Lord *your God, who rescued you from slavery in the land of Egypt. Do not forget that he led you through the great and terrifying wilderness with its poisonous snakes and scorpions, where it was so hot and dry. He gave you water from the rock! He fed you with manna in the wilderness, a food unknown to your ancestors. He did this to humble you and test you for your own good. He did all this so you would never say to yourself, "I have achieved this wealth with my own strength and energy."*
>
> (Deuteronomy 8:11–17 NLT)

Seven hundred years later, God's people had forgotten His commands, had ignored His Word, had pursued their own agendas and comfort, and were poised to face the consequences of their actions.

> *"The time is surely coming," says the Sovereign* Lord, *"when I will send a famine on the land—not a famine of bread or water but of hearing the words of the* Lord.*"*
>
> (Amos 8:11 NLT)

The prophet Amos told them that because they had forgotten God, they were going to suffer a famine. But it would not be an ordinary famine of food and water. This famine would be far worse because it would mean that their God would become silent toward them. This famine would be one of silence—the inability to hear God's voice of truth and counsel.

You may read these words and think, *Wow! That doesn't seem so bad. At least they still had food, shelter, and all the rest of the abundance that God had given them. How bad could it be for God to be silent to them for a while?*

For the nation of Israel, it was devastating. This was a people who, whether they knew it or not, depended on God's guidance. Beginning with Moses, the Israelites had been blessed with several dependable leaders who would hear from God and point them in the right direction. Whenever they had strayed from God's path and experienced suffering due to their own disobedience, God had always raised up a leader to help them correct their course.

When God told Israel that they would suffer a famine *"of hearing the words of the LORD,"* it meant, in effect, that they would be condemned to a future of confusion, failure, and defeat.

Starving in the Midst of Abundance

Today, many individuals, families, and even congregations are suffering their own famine of God's Word. This may sound absurd, especially given the massive amounts of teaching and resources that American Christians have at their disposal. Today, we are blessed with a nearly unlimited supply of Bibles, inspirational books, CDs, DVDs, and other resources on nearly every conceivable topic. We have access to Christian Web sites by the thousands, as well as Christian radio and television, offering wisdom from the very best teachers and preachers in the world. In many communities, there are weekly meetings, seminars, and other opportunities to study and know what God is saying to us on many levels. In short, compared to our parents' and grandparents' generations—and especially compared to other nations around the world—we have daily opportunities to enjoy a veritable feast of God's life-transforming Word.

Through busyness, the cares of this world, attention to other interests, and the pursuit of luxury and ease, many of God's people are robbing themselves of the true riches that God has for them.

Then, why is it that many Christians today seem so unseasoned in the ways of God? Why are many individuals and families walking in confusion and bondage, things the Bible says they should be free from? Why are so many people ignorant of even the most basic elements of the Christian faith? The answer is that they are not accessing God's Word for themselves. It is nothing less than a self-imposed famine. Through busyness, the cares of this world, attention to other interests, and the pursuit of luxury and ease, many of God's people are robbing themselves of the true riches that God has for them.

The prophet Amos witnessed a similar state of affairs in his own day. As he looked around him, this humble man of God was grieved to see his fellow citizens consumed by their own pursuits, trying to get ahead, living for luxury, blind to God's warning that such behavior and attitudes would cripple them spiritually and lead their nation into a state of deep jeopardy.

Again, in America, we are rapidly changing from the "land of the free and the home of the brave" to a nation of self-centered people who are drowning in debt, living for pleasure, and consumed by the cares of this world. This is, I believe, what Jesus was referring to when He related the parable of the sower in Luke 8. In it, He taught about good seed being sown in different kinds of soil, yielding different results.

Now the [seeds] *that fell among thorns are those who, when they have heard, go out and are choked with cares, riches, and pleasures of life, and bring no fruit to maturity.* (Luke 8:14)

Many Christians today are like the seeds sown among thorns. They hear God's Word on a regular basis, and they may even receive it with joy, but, inwardly, the eternal truths they hear have very little impact on them because their lives are consumed by earthly cares and the pursuit of riches and pleasure.

Do you see yourself fitting this description? Do you have a deep desire to love and serve God but at the same time, find yourself bound by the things of this world? In the book of Revelation, Jesus warned the church what would happen if they did not firmly and emphatically turn from their double-mindedness: *"Because you are lukewarm, and neither cold nor hot, I will vomit you out of My mouth"* (Revelation 3:16).

You might find such an ultimatum surprising coming from a God who declares that He loves all people and does not want any to perish. But those who fit such a description are of no use to the kingdom of God because they never come to maturity. They are spiritual weaklings because the things of this world prevent them from feeding regularly on God's Word, the only thing that has value. In the end, they find it impossible to declare their total allegiance to the Lord Jesus Christ.

Moral and Spiritual Compromise

The apostle Paul emphasized the importance of God's people remaining upright in their behavior and lifestyle: *"Don't team up with those who are unbelievers. How can righteousness be a partner with wickedness? How can light live with darkness?"* (2 Corinthians 6:14 NLT). Christians are called to be the light of Christ in this world. Instead of being the light, however, many Christians find themselves compromising their faith and embracing the same dark lifestyles as the unsaved—watching the same filthy, violent movies and television shows, listening to the same demonically motivated music, and practicing the same behaviors that lead away from the light. Ask yourself: *Am I allowing things into my house via the Internet, magazines, DVDs, music, and other media that will spiritually harm me or my family?*

Instead of being salt and light that will change the world through the love of Christ, many Christians have allowed themselves to be changed by the world. They have let the standard of this world become their own standard, ignoring the only standard that has any meaning or relevance: God's Word. We must come back to the Word of the Lord. *"Therefore, come out from among unbelievers, and separate yourselves from them, says the LORD. Don't touch their filthy things, and I will welcome you"* (2 Corinthians 6:17 NLT).

The only way back to having strong churches and strong families is through God's Word working mightily in our hearts and lives. The writer of Hebrews compared God's Word to a sharp sword that is able to cut to the heart of the issues in our lives that need to be dealt with.

> *For the word of God is living and powerful, and sharper than any two-edged sword, piercing even to the division of soul and spirit, and of joints and marrow, and is a discerner of the thoughts and intents of the heart.*
>
> (Hebrews 4:12)

In order to resist the world and become the light of Christ to others, we need to allow God the freedom to do the necessary surgery on our hearts.

Back to a Reverence for God

Today, I believe that we are standing at a crossroads in the spiritual life of America, as well as in the survival of our families. One way will lead us down a path of continued destruction, forsaking God's counsel concerning compromise with the world. The other way—the one Jesus called *"narrow"* (Matthew 7:13–14; Luke 13:24)—will lead our families, churches, communities, and nation back to the mercy and abundance God has promised through His Son.

To be on that path of life and blessing requires two heart conditions:

1. Deep reverence for God

2. Faith in God's Word

Reverence for God—which the Bible also calls *"the fear of the LORD"* (Proverbs 9:10)—is the very foundation for the wisdom and knowledge we need to find the success and destiny for which God created us. Proverbs tells us that living with a reverence for God will ensure that He protects and guides our every step.

The fear of the LORD leads to life, and he who has it will abide in satisfaction; he will not be visited with evil.
(Proverbs 19:23)

Many Christians whom I meet today need to come back to a healthy fear of God. They have spent too much time on the fence, trying to live as God's children while still pursuing a lifestyle they know is displeasing to Him. The fear of God—a deep reverence and desire to please Him in all our ways—brings with it a motivation to turn from evil. It also brings a desire to know God more, which will, in turn, lead us back to His Word. And when we get back into the Word of God, the famine will end, and our faith in Him will grow again.

> **The fear of God—a deep reverence and desire to please Him in all our ways—brings with it a motivation to turn from evil.**

The way back to reverence and fear of God requires that all of us take a serious look at our lives, allowing the Holy Spirit to shine His searchlight into every area, showing us where we need to repent of sinful behavior and experience transformation. We need to pray as King David did:

Search me, O God, and know my heart; test me and know my anxious thoughts. Point out anything in me that offends you, and lead me along the path of everlasting life. (Psalm 139:23–24 NLT)

Ending the Famine

Now is the time to turn back to God, to end the famine of hearing His Word, and to return to having strong, spiritually vibrant churches and families. As the apostle Paul said, *"Faith comes by hearing, and hearing by the word of God"* (Romans 10:17).

When hearing and heeding take root within us, God's Word becomes powerful in our lives. Jesus said, *"The words that I speak to you are spirit, and they are life"* (John 6:63). If His words abide in you—if you hear them and take them to heart— then God's Holy Spirit will empower you to live in the true victory and abundance that Christ died and rose again to give you.

God wants us to love His Word because, when we do, we fall more and more in love with Him. That, of course, is the whole reason He created us. In fact, He commanded us to love Him with all of our heart, soul, mind, and strength. (See Mark 12:30.) In other words, we must love the Lord aggressively and emphatically, making Him our number one priority in life. That will happen only by loving His Word because that is the only way we can truly know the character and person of our Lord.

Perhaps nobody represented in Scripture loved God's Word more than King David. He put a high priority on it because he knew that out of it flowed all the wisdom and knowledge he needed for life. As the psalmist declared, *"Oh, how I love Your law! It is my meditation all the day"* (Psalm 119:97).

David gave us a wealth of understanding about the value of God's Word.

> *The law of the Lord is perfect, converting the soul; the testimony of the Lord is sure, making wise the simple; the statutes of the Lord are right, rejoicing the heart; the commandment of the Lord is pure, enlightening the eyes; the fear of the Lord is clean, enduring forever; the judgments of the Lord are true and righteous altogether.*
> (Psalm 19:7–9)

According to this passage, God's Word...

- is able to convert our souls.
- is able to make us wise.
- is able to bring great joy to our hearts.
- gives us necessary insight for our life's journey.

- never changes.
- is the absolute measuring stick for truth and righteousness.

David went on to declare that God's Word is *"more to be desired...than gold, yea, than much fine gold; sweeter also than honey and the honeycomb"* (Psalm 19:10).

Make the Choice!

How would you like to have that kind of passion for God's Word? How would your life be changed if you developed an absolute love of God's Word and made it of higher importance than any other priority or possession in your life? That doesn't happen by accident. It happens intentionally when you ask God for a hunger for His Word and His ways. It happens when you ask God for an ever-deeper intimacy with Him and for a stripping away from your life of the things of this world.

I want to invite you to make such a pursuit the cry of your heart. It will change you personally, transform your family, and make you a key "mover and shaker" in regard to seeing revival and transformation come to your church, your community, and your nation.

Would you pray the following prayer, making it a personal request to your heavenly Father, in order to complete a lasting work within you?

> Father, I ask that You would give me a deep and abiding desire for Your life-changing and eternal Word, so that knowing You, loving You, and seeing Your kingdom come and Your will accomplished would become my sole motivation in life. Lord, transform me and my family, church, neighborhood, community, and nation through Your Word of life. In Jesus' name I pray, amen.

Chapter Ten

A Foundation in Crisis

There is little argument today that many of the foundations that are crucial to a strong, stable society are under attack as never before. Nowhere has this been more evident than in the ongoing assault against traditional families in America. At one time, it was clearly understood that a key building block of any prosperous, productive, and strong society was the family unit—consisting of one man, one woman, and their children. Unfortunately, such an understanding no longer seems to be the case. In fact, the traditional ideas of marriage and family have become a prime target of those who would like to equate these sacred institutions with alternative lifestyles, such as homosexual relationships and other morally destructive behaviors.

In his book *God, Marriage, and Family: Rebuilding the Biblical Foundation*, Andreas J. Köstenberger notes that in today's chaotic political and social atmosphere,

> ...for the first time in its history, Western civilization is confronted with the need to define the meaning of the terms "marriage" and "family." What until now has been considered a "normal" family, made up of a father, a mother, and a number of children, has in recent years increasingly begun to be viewed as one among several options, which can no longer claim to be the only or even superior form of ordering human relationships. The Judeo-Christian view of marriage and the family with its roots in the Hebrew Scriptures has to a certain extent been replaced with a set of values that prizes human rights, self-fulfillment, and pragmatic utility on an

individual and societal level. It can rightly be said that marriage and the family are institutions under siege in our world today, and that with marriage and the family, our very civilization is in crisis.[22]

The family is the nucleus of civilization. —Will Durant

An Ongoing Assault

Marriage and family have been under intense assault for many years, and not just from those who would like to see these God-ordained institutions reconfigured to include the sanctioning of morally reprehensible lifestyles. Over the last several decades, as our society has drifted from the conservative Judeo-Christian morals of previous generations and embraced an increasingly liberal attitude toward sex and marriage, the consequences to families have been catastrophic. As early as the 1970s, for many young couples, the appeal of a lifetime commitment of marriage began to be replaced by the option of cohabitation—a kind of "trial marriage." With the absence of an aggressive challenge to this behavior from the church, the institution of marriage began to crumble as, over the decades, more and more children were born into "families" in which Mommy and Daddy were not married, Daddy had left home, or nobody was quite sure just who Daddy was in the first place.

Today, an alarming number of children are raised in single-parent homes. According to the 2000 U.S. Census, 40 percent of American families with children under the age of eighteen were single-parent families. In 1970, that number was only 13 percent. And research shows that six out of ten children under the age of eighteen will live in a single-parent home at some point in their childhoods, with single mothers heading nine of ten single-parent families.

Even among Christians, marriage and family are not immune to attack. Research shows that marriages among Christians are as prone to end in divorce as marriages among non-Christians. In a 2008 study, George Barna found that among "born-again" Christians—those who claim to have a personal relationship with Jesus Christ and say that their faith is important to them—the rate of divorce is 32 percent, nearly as high as the rate among non-Christians.[23]

While today's young parents hope that their children will not face the same pain of shattered marriages that many of them suffered through, the current trend does not offer a great deal of hope. Writes Barna,

> Interviews with young adults suggest that they want their initial marriage to last, but are not particularly optimistic about that possibility. There is also evidence that many young people are moving toward embracing the idea of serial marriage, in which a person gets married two or three times, seeking a different partner for each phase of their adult life.[24]

Has the mold been set for the future of marriage and family? Are we looking at the demise of one of the institutions that is most important to the survival of sane society? What can we do to reverse the trend and once again build marriages and families that can survive the storms of modern life?

> The foundations of civilization are no stronger and no more enduring than the corporate integrity of the homes on which they rest. If the homes deteriorate, civilization will crumble and fall.   —Billy Graham

Back to the Biblical Model

For the sake of our children and for future generations, we must turn back to the model that establishes strong families: God's model. We must repent where we have fallen away from God's truth. We must teach it to our children so that they can know and follow God's plan for marriage and family.

As members of the church—those who have been washed in the blood of Jesus Christ and are growing in His likeness—we are not to be *"unequally yoked"* (2 Corinthians 6:14) with the lifestyles of people who do not know God. He calls us to separate ourselves from behaviors that are contrary to His will and ways. Of course, that does not mean we should reject those who do not know Christ. But we *are* to reject lifestyles and worldviews that contradict His call to absolute holiness in our lives.

When God brought the children of Israel out of Egypt and established them as His people, He gave them specific directions and commandments that were to ensure their success in every area of life. Supreme among those commandments was the charge to *"love the Lord your God with all your heart, with all your soul, and with all your strength"* (Deuteronomy 6:5). This was nonnegotiable—and still is to this day.

In too many Christian homes, however, loving God is not a priority. Instead, money, career, success, possessions, and recreation have taken priority above God. The result has been dramatic. Rebellion among children is rampant. Pornography, drug addiction, adultery, lying, stealing, anger, and abuse are occurring way too frequently in households that claim to call upon the name of Jesus Christ. The media barrage that confessing Christians allow into their homes through television, movies, music, and the Internet is heartbreaking.

> In too many Christian homes, loving God is not a priority. Instead, money, career, success, possessions, and recreation have taken priority above God.

And this is all due to the fact that many Christians have not allowed God's Holy Spirit to transform their attitudes into ones that would make Him their inheritance, their love, and their life. They have not allowed God's unchanging truth to be the measuring stick in their marriages and families.

Keeping His Word in Our Hearts and Homes

How can we return to being families that honor God? How do we raise children who are strong and committed to one another? We have to give heed to God's Word, and we must make sure that our children know and honor His truths, as well.

In Deuteronomy 6, God made this clear to the people of Israel.

> *And these words which I command you today shall be in your heart. You shall teach them diligently to your children, and shall talk of them when you sit in your house, when you walk by the way, when you lie down, and when you rise up. You shall bind them as a sign on your hand, and they shall be as frontlets between your eyes.* (Deuteronomy 6:6–8)

They were to talk about God's Word to their children both day and night. In fact, God's transforming Word was to be so important to them that they were to write it on the very doorposts of their homes.

We must teach our children the ways of God through our lifestyles, through Bible-believing, God-honoring churches, and through regular times spent together as families in the Word and in prayer. By the way, this is not new advice. Proverbs 22:6 instructs us to *"train up a child in the way he should go, and when he is old he will not depart from it."* Our children will become the next generation that honors and loves God. That is how we rebuild strong families.

Let's take a look at God's model for the family unit.

In the Beginning

> *What God has joined together, let not man separate.* (Matthew 19:6)

One of God's most beautiful and profoundly impactful acts of creation occurred when He took one of Adam's ribs and used it to create the woman, Eve. (See Genesis 2:21–25.) This was the beginning of the family unit. It demonstrated the necessity of the two founding members—man and woman—to the success of the family. Nature itself bears witness to the truth that without a man and a woman coming together, there can be no offspring. Thus, we have the true definition of a family. While it is true that there are all sorts of groupings of people who call themselves a "family," in truth, it takes a man and a woman, coming together as *"one flesh"* (Genesis 2:24; Matthew 19:5–6; Mark 10:8; 1 Corinthians 6:16; Ephesians 5:31) in marriage to compose the God-ordained family unit.

Our modern culture has so diminished this intimacy between a man and a woman that many view it as nothing more than a recreational activity, with sex being equated with the pornographic, the lewd, and the basest instincts of human beings. This, of course, was never God's intent. His design is for a man and a woman to come together in the commitment of love, to leave their mother and father, and to cling to one another for the duration of their earthly lives. Nothing could be more beautiful, inspiring, and productive in this world than love, marriage, and family as God designed them.

Now is the time for God's people to return to His design, forsaking the cheap and tawdry imitations that the world has to offer.

In the very beginning, God laid out the model for marriage and family:

> *A man shall leave his father and mother and be joined to his wife, and they shall become one flesh.*
>
> (Genesis 2:24)

Marriage begins when a man takes the initiative to leave his old family unit—father, mother, and siblings—to commit himself to one woman for the rest of his life. Jesus quoted this very passage from Genesis to emphasize the divinely ordained nature of traditional marriage when He said:

> *Have you not read that He who made them at the beginning "made them male and female," and said, "For this reason a man shall leave his father and mother and be*

joined to his wife, and the two shall become one flesh"?
So then, they are no longer two but one flesh. Therefore
what God has joined together, let not man separate.
(Matthew 19:4–6)

Notice Jesus' bold statement to emphasize the importance of this family unit before God Almighty: *"What God has joined together, let not man separate."*

In this day of easy "no-fault" divorce, when multiple marriages—even among Christians—are common and accepted, and when the very definition of marriage has become whatever a majority of individuals defines it as being, what would happen if God's people took to heart His view on marriage and family and insisted in their own homes, churches, and communities on honoring God and taking His Word seriously? That is the only way we are going to be able to turn the tide of failing families and avoid the very destruction of our society.

Remember what God declared in 2 Chronicles 7:14:

If My people who are called by My name will humble
themselves, and pray and seek My face, and turn from
their wicked ways, then I will hear from heaven, and
will forgive their sin and heal their land.

> **Too many of God's people are bound in chains that this world has convinced them are normal and standard operating procedure for everyone.**

This is God's promise to heal our homes, our families, our communities, and even our nation. But it will take not only *hearing* God's Word but also intentionally choosing to *obey* and *follow* His commands and ways. Jesus said, *"If you abide in My word, you are My disciples indeed. And you shall know the truth, and the truth shall make you free"* (John 8:31–32).

Unfortunately, too many of God's people are bound in chains that this world has convinced them are normal and standard operating procedure for everyone. The only way for each and every one of us to break the hold of that bondage is to take a stand for righteousness—a right standard of conduct and attitude of our hearts. That, of course, begins with acknowledging Christ as Savior, and it continues by making Him Lord of our hearts and our homes.

As for me and my house, we will serve the LORD.
(Joshua 24:15)

"As for Me and My House...."

Toward the end of his life, the great Hebrew leader Joshua put a challenge before the children of Israel to walk uprightly in the midst of a world that largely rejected God. His words are just as relevant to us today as we walk in a world filled with chaos, rebellion, sin, immorality, and disobedience to God's righteous standard. God had blessed His people with a Promised Land of awesome opportunity—a *"land flowing with milk and honey"* (Deuteronomy 31:20). But it was also a land filled with other nations of people who walked contrary to the Word of God. The previous generation of Israelites had allowed themselves to be corrupted. Instead of following God, they had worshipped the false gods and idols of Egypt. Once in the wilderness, they complained and even made their own golden calf to worship. At the very doorstep of the Promised Land, they chose to believe reports of giants in the land rather than the more optimistic and faithful reports of Caleb and Joshua. They allowed fear to sap their faith in the promises of God. Because of their lack of faith, God forbid them from entering into this new land.

Do not harden your hearts, as in the rebellion, as in the day of trial in the wilderness, when your fathers tested Me; they tried Me, though they saw My work. For forty years I was grieved with that generation, and said, "It is a people who go astray in their hearts, and they do not know My ways." So I swore in My wrath, "They shall not enter My rest." (Psalm 95:8–11)

As the elderly Joshua faced his own death, he warned this new generation, *"Put away the gods which your fathers served on the other side of the River and in Egypt. Serve the LORD!"* (Joshua 24:14).

Then, Joshua made this thought-provoking challenge:

Choose for yourselves this day whom you will serve, whether the gods which your fathers served that were on the other side of the River, or the gods of the Amorites, in whose land you dwell. But as for me and my house, we will serve the LORD. (verse 15)

Joshua's declaration to the children of Israel stands also as a declaration and challenge to the church of today—to those of us who struggle with the influences of the godless culture that surrounds us and denies God and His ways.

Stand in the Gap

Is Joshua's declaration one you can make for your own family? It matters not how large or small your household. You may lead a family that includes your children and your children's children, or you may be a family of "empty nesters" whose children have moved on and started families of their own. Or, perhaps you are a solitary individual with no one but yourself to call "family." Maybe you're not even the head of a household, but you have a deep desire to see your family members love God and follow Him. Whatever the size of the household, and whatever your place in it, you have the privilege and the responsibility to declare before the rest of the world, *"As for me and my house, we will serve the LORD."*

You can make that declaration through your lifestyle, your words, and your prayers—day in and day out—for God's mercy and blessing on your family. God is looking for individuals who will stand in the gap for their families, diligently praying on a daily basis that husbands, wives, children, and grandchildren will walk before the Lord humbly and with pure hearts. A return to strong families who love the Lord with all their hearts, souls, minds, and strength begins with mothers, fathers, grandparents, children, and grandchildren praying for transformation, revival, and God's touch on their lives.

In other words, it begins with you. Here is a note I received recently from a woman in our church named Stephanie who stood in the gap for her daughter:

> *I want to thank our heavenly Father, for He has truly answered my prayers. I had been praying to God for the safe return of my daughter who was out on the streets. I had no idea of her whereabouts. I remained in prayer and in God's Word, not giving up, and knowing my prayers would prevail and the enemy would be defeated.*
>
> *Yesterday, as I was praying, God gave me a vision of white clouds and a white double door. As I opened the door in my vision, there was my daughter. I grabbed her and began to hug her. Later, I shared my vision with my husband, my mother, and my brother. I told all of them that my daughter was coming home that very day.*
>
> *That afternoon, as I was getting ready for a wedding, my cell phone rang. It was my daughter. She asked me what I was doing and I informed her I was getting ready to go to a wedding. She said she was ready to come home. In that moment, I began to thank Jesus. I told her I would not go to the wedding but would go and pick her up, and that's what I did.*
>
> *God is so good! I love Him so much! He is my Provider, and I will continue to stay in faith, believing and trusting in Him always. He is my on-time God! I thank the church for praying for me and ask that you all continue to lift me in prayer for my family and finances. May God continue to bless your ministry and all you do in the name of Jesus.*

There is no situation so dire that it cannot be laid at God's feet in prayer. You are never too young or too old to intercede for your family. If you have no family, you are a prime candidate to spend your time lifting up all the other families in your neighborhood, asking God to save them, change them, and make them strong in the face of every storm of life so that they, too, will declare, *"As for me and my house, we will serve the Lord."*

Chapter Eleven

A Return to Strong Families

The ongoing assault on families in America has been well documented over the last thirty-plus years. I am convinced that the roots of this disintegration began more than sixty years ago, with the end of World War II and the beginning of a period of unprecedented prosperity in our nation.

Before World War II, many Americans grew up with little or nothing as their families struggled through the Great Depression. Hardly had they reached adulthood when their nation was thrust into war and millions of young men were called to serve their country. Those who remained at home provided much of the industrial manpower that created the goods and equipment that supplied the troops. As they did so, they faced a wartime economy with the rationing of food, fuel, and other necessities. At the end of the war, an army of young men came home to resume their lives, while the nation's economy responded by blossoming into a time of prosperity and abundance during a period of relative peace.

But something began to change as a hungry and motivated nation eagerly pursued the "American Dream." Throughout the 1950s and 60s, as Dad worked hard in order to purchase a home, a new automobile, and all the things that Madison Avenue convinced his family they needed, he found himself spending less and less time on the thing that really mattered: the family he was working diligently to support.

"Leanness into Their Soul"

As prosperity and abundance multiplied, and the nation's standard of living skyrocketed, there also came a *"leanness into their soul"* (Psalm 106:15). For many people, faith in God was slowly replaced with the love for, and pursuit of, wealth, possessions, recreation, and social status. While previous generations had placed a high priority on spiritual values, many among the post-war generation of Americans thought about their relationship with God less and less. As a result, many of their children and their children's children grew up knowing little of God's love, justice, and standards for their lives.

For many, the pursuit of wealth and self-fulfillment became a religion unto itself. It is little wonder, then, that America's homes have become increasingly unfriendly—even emotionally toxic—to children. The statistics tell a sad story:

- Fewer than half of America's children grow up in families where both mother and father are present.

- Since 2000, there has been a dramatic increase in child abuse serious enough to be labeled as "violent."

- Each day in this country, 2,800 teenage girls become pregnant.[25]

- Each day, 1,106 teen mothers-to-be end the lives of their unborn babies through abortion.[26]

- In 2004, the Centers for Disease Control and Prevention reported that the suicide rate in American adolescents (ages 10 to 24) increased 8 percent, to a rate of 7.32 per 100,000 people that age.[27] This was the largest one-year increase in suicides in fifteen years. Experts estimate that for every successful suicide, there are ten more teens who attempt and fail.

- By the time they graduate from high school, 54 percent of our nation's teens acknowledge that they have used one or more illegal drugs.[28]

What Makes a Solid Family?

We are living in a time of great stress for families, and many homes are breaking down under increasing financial, emotional, and spiritual pressures. But it is also true that we are living in a time when strong, close-knit families are one of the only safe havens in a world of increasing chaos and darkness.

In 1977, authors-researchers Dr. Nick Stinnett and Dr. John DeFrain launched a study to determine the keys to families in which the husband and wife were happily married and had strong and stable relationships with their children. They interviewed three thousand families from diverse backgrounds and ethnicities and found that the strongest families—those that were the happiest and best adjusted—shared these six key characteristics:

1. Family members were committed to each other.

2. Family members enjoyed spending time together.

3. Family members had good communication with each other.

4. Family members openly expressed their love and appreciation of each other.

5. Family members had a spiritual commitment.

6. Family members maintained cohesive, close relationships with one another in crisis situations.[29]

What would happen if moms and dads committed to cultivating these types of characteristics in their families and households? Such a task would not be easy, but it would not be impossible, either. I believe that such a commitment to change, made individually by each family, is crucial to the type of turnaround that will transform our country into a strong, God-fearing nation once again. Furthermore, I believe there are some additional keys that will help families gain the strength to stand under whatever stresses the world throws at them.

Are You a "Revolutionary Parent"?

In his highly informative and challenging book *Revolutionary Parenting: What the Research Shows Really Works* (Barna Books, 2007), George Barna identified three types of parenting styles that predominate in American society today, and he analyzed how these styles impact the types of children raised. The three styles are:

Parenting by Default

This is what Barna calls parenting by "the path of least resistance." Mom and Dad do whatever is most convenient and natural, based on the cultural norms and traditions that are in fashion at the time. "The objective is to keep everyone—parent, child, and others—as happy as possible, without having the process of parenting dominate other important or prioritized aspects of the parent's life," noted Barna.[30]

Trial-and-Error Parenting

Barna explained that this style is based on the idea that there are no absolute guidelines for effective parenting, and parents improve their child-rearing skills through experimentation. "In this incremental approach, the goals of parenting are to continually improve and to perform better than most other parents."[31]

Revolutionary Parenting

This is, by far, the least common approach to parenting, requiring parents "to take God's words on life and family at face value, and to apply those words faithfully and consistently."[32]

It doesn't take a family expert to identify which of the above parenting styles is most likely to facilitate the rearing of children who are grounded in their faith, focused on their life's purpose, and wired with a sense of personal responsibility toward God and others.

Coming from the point of view that God created each human being for an eternal spiritual purpose, Barna established a handful of core standards overwhelmingly exhibited by young people whose parents were faithful to incorporate God's Word and the fundamentals of faith in their daily family life. Among other things, each of the young adults in the study:

- Believed that a top priority in life was knowing, loving, and serving God

- Said his or her faith in God was of the highest importance in life

- Exhibited a worldview founded upon, among other tenets, a belief in absolute moral truth, as defined in the Bible, the existence of God as the all-powerful Creator and Ruler of the universe, and faith in Jesus Christ as Savior and Lord

- Placed importance on active participation in a vibrant community of faith—a church—and consistently engaged in worship, prayer, Bible study, and spiritual accountability

If you are like me, you may look at the core standards embraced by these young adults and think to yourself, *Is it even possible to successfully raise this type of kid today?* With all of the distractions, chaos, wickedness, and enemy activity in our culture, many parents are just trying to maintain a semblance of order and basic moral sanity in their homes. Their goal has gone from raising kids with spiritual focus and momentum to merely raising kids who have not been too badly tainted by the things of this world.

God's mercy and transforming power are far bigger than our perceived limitations to effective parenting and sound families.

Nevertheless, I am convinced that God's mercy and transforming power are far bigger than our perceived limitations to effective parenting and sound families. After all, as the apostle Paul assured us, not only is it God's great pleasure for each of us to be an integral part of His kingdom through Jesus Christ, but He Himself takes the initiative to make it happen. (See Philippians 2:13.)

As families make a commitment to see God's glory abide in their homes, and as parents make the commitment to pray for their children to become all that God created them to be, our heavenly Father is faithful to create something beautiful and fruitful in our lives. He works beyond our faults, our failures, and our inadequacies as He answers the cries of our hearts to be men, women, children, and yes, families that will honor Him on this earth.

Fathers Are Key

The Bible is clear on the roles that mother, father, and children play in the family. If we as parents will prayerfully seek to make sure that each family member is fulfilling his or her God-ordained role, our Father will meet us and give us the success He has promised!

If there is one family member who is the key to the overall spiritual success of all other family members, it is the father. What do you suppose has been the number one issue that has impacted families and children in America, and one that continues to be a major problem? It is a home that lacks a father.

As I mentioned previously, the 2000 U.S. Census Bureau figures show that two out of every five children in America will live in a single-parent home before they reach the age of eighteen. In fact, as recently as 2002, around twenty million children were living in such households—more than 25 percent of all American children. The vast majority of those children were living in homes with no fathers.

In the 1970s and 80s, as divorce became prevalent in our society, children began to lose their fathers as their parents split up. While such situations were certainly unfortunate, at least many of those children knew and saw their fathers through joint-custody and other arrangements between their parents. Sadly, this is less and less the case today. Most single-parent children have mothers who were never married to their fathers and, in many cases, do not know who their fathers are.

The problem is obvious: fathers are abandoning their God-ordained responsibilities to raise their children, and the consequences could not be more dire. Here are the sad facts:

- 63 percent of children and adolescents who commit suicide come from fatherless homes. (U.S. Department of Health and Human Services, Bureau of the Census)

- 71 percent of pregnant teens are from homes lacking fathers. (U.S.D.H.H.S. press release, Friday, March 26, 1999)

- 90 percent of homeless and runaway children come from fatherless homes. (U.S.D.H.H.S., Bureau of the Census)

- 70 percent of incarcerated youth come from fatherless homes. (U.S. Department of Justice report, September 1988)

- 85 percent of children exhibiting some sort of behavioral disorder come from homes lacking fathers. (United States Center for Disease Control)

- 71 percent of America's high school dropouts are from homes with no fathers. (National Principals Association Report on the State of High Schools, 1998)

- 75 percent of prisoners in the U.S. came from homes lacking fathers. (Daniel Amneus, *The Garbage Generation*, Alhambra, CA: Primrose Press, 1990)

Are you beginning to see the pattern?

The problems in our nation cannot be blamed solely on crime, juvenile delinquency, unemployment, ineffective school systems, drug and alcohol abuse, poor governmental programs, or other socioeconomic pathologies. Those things are symptoms of a bigger problem: broken homes and shattered families. And a large part of that problem can be laid at the feet of men who have not lived up to their God-given responsibility in the family.

Love the Lord, Then Your Family

I realize that it is not fashionable or politically correct to suggest that God has established different realms of authority for men and women in His kingdom. Such talk flies in the face of the type of feminism that has dominated our culture for the past few decades. Of course, Scripture is clear that God shows no favoritism in His acceptance and love for people, regardless of gender, race, ethnicity, or any other delineation. The apostle Paul told us that *"there is neither Jew nor Greek, there is neither slave nor free, there is neither male nor female; for you are all one in Christ Jesus"* (Galatians 3:28).

But Scripture is also clear that God commissions specific individuals in His kingdom with certain authorities and duties, and in the home—composed of a husband, wife, and children—the father's headship and authority are clear. Men, you were created to take the spiritual headship in your families.

> *For the husband is head of the wife, as also Christ is head of the church; and He is the Savior of the body. Therefore, just as the church is subject to Christ, so let the wives be to their own husbands in everything.*
> (Ephesians 5:23–24)

Men, you are to love your wives as Christ loved the church. You are to lead your children into a lifelong relationship with Jesus Christ.

Now, many wives and mothers may read this and think, *My home certainly doesn't work like that. In fact, if it weren't for my spiritual input into our family, there would be no Christian leadership at all.* The sad truth is that in far too many homes and families, men have abandoned their role as spiritual head, and it has fallen instead to wives, mothers, grandmothers, and other women to cover the family in prayer and spiritual authority.

That is not God's design. Scripture is clear that men are to take the lead in raising children who love God and in guiding their households in faith. And, men, it all begins with a pattern of spiritual behavior in your personal life.

As we saw in the last chapter, the greatest commandment in Scripture is

The sad truth is that in far too many homes and families, men have abandoned their role as spiritual head, and it has fallen instead to wives, mothers, grandmothers, and other women to cover the family in prayer and spiritual authority.

to love the Lord God with your heart, soul, mind, and strength. Moses gave this command from God, not just for the children of Israel to obey, but for every individual and every household. Jesus repeated this command and then included another with it:

> *"You shall love the LORD your God with all your heart, with all your soul, and with all your mind." This is the first and great commandment. And the second is like it: "You shall love your neighbor as yourself."*
>   (Matthew 22:37–39)

If there is one thing we all struggle with, it is selfishness. We have no trouble loving ourselves and putting ourselves first. But loving others is a different matter. If we aren't holding a grudge or being critical of someone else, we often find ourselves putting the needs of others behind our own. But that was not the way with Jesus. He always loved—and still loves—with the same passion that God loves. And, men, as we see in Scripture, that is your role, as well: loving God first, your families second, and yourselves last. Placing your family and their needs above your own desires is the first step in taking the headship of your family that God requires.

Loving and serving your children means tenderly, patiently bringing them up in the ways of God. In fact, in Ephesians, the apostle Paul counseled fathers not to be unkind and harsh to their children, making them angry and resentful with rigid, abusive treatment and standards they could never reach.

> *Fathers, do not provoke your children to wrath, but bring them up in the training and admonition of the Lord.*
>   (Ephesians 6:4)

Being harsh and unkind will serve only to foster rebellion and disobedience—the opposite of what we really want to cultivate in our kids. Instead, God calls you to bring up your children with loving instruction and fair discipline, just as He does with you. The Bible is clear that God is merciful, patient, and kind—three main qualities your kids should see in you.

Make Your Instruction Intentional

There is a follow-up to God's command to love Him above everything else.

You shall teach [God's commandments] *diligently to your children, and shall talk of them when you sit in your house, when you walk by the way, when you lie down, and when you rise up.* (Deuteronomy 6:7)

Wherever we go with our children, we are to look for opportunities to talk to them about God, teaching His Word and ways to them.

Men, how many of you are intentional in spending time with your kids, teaching them how to love God? There are so many things that can get in the way of that on any given day. There's golf with your buddies and yard work, not to mention the big game on Sunday afternoon. I know from experience that even when we spend time with our kids, the activities we choose can either contribute to talking about spiritual things or pull us away from our best intentions. But if you will prayerfully stay attuned to God's voice as you spend time with your kids, you will find awesome opportunities to teach them God's Word. And, believe me, the Word of God that you help them hide in their hearts today will stay with them long after they have grown.

I am convinced that if we, as Christian parents, will spend quality time with our kids, teaching them what the Word of God says and how it can transform their lives, we will spend a lot less time disciplining them.

All Scripture is given by inspiration of God, and is profitable for doctrine, for reproof, for correction, for instruction in righteousness, that the man of God may be complete, thoroughly equipped for every good work. (2 Timothy 3:16–17)

Dads, there is no greater duty—or privilege—that God has given you than to do all you can to make sure that when your children walk out the door of your home to make their ways in this world, they will do so as young men and women who love God and are thoroughly grounded in His Word.

"Husbands, Love Your Wives"

As important as it is for fathers to take the lead in teaching their children to love God, I believe that there is an even more important duty that men have as husbands and fathers. It is a command straight from the heart of God, and it is foundational to the spiritual fiber of our families.

> *Husbands, love your wives, just as Christ also loved the church and gave Himself for her, that He might sanctify and cleanse her with the washing of water by the word.* (Ephesians 5:25–26)

If we want our families to be transformed and strengthened in a way that will also transform our churches, our communities, and our nation, it must begin with the simple act of husbands loving their wives.

Husbands are to love their wives. It is that simple. If we want our families to be transformed and strengthened in a way that will also transform our churches, our communities, and our nation, it must begin with the simple act of husbands loving their wives.

And how is a husband to do that? This Scripture passage makes it clear that the husband is to love his wife as Christ loved the church. And how did Christ love the church? He laid down His life for it, pouring out His heavenly Father's compassion, mercy, and forgiveness. He gave His all for each and every one of us, thinking of our needs, of God's destiny for us, and of what He could do to make sure we fulfilled our God-given purpose.

Yet very little of that kind of love seems to exist in our homes and families today! Instead, many of us are so intent on pursuing our own agendas and seeking our own fulfillment that we forget anyone else exists. Men, Jesus is your example, and if you are serious about being conformed to His image, the number one way to do that is through loving others. And that begins with loving your wife as Christ loved His own bride, the church. It means pouring out your life for her—being a servant. This kind of posture completely removes any possibility of using your headship in an abusive, controlling, or manipulative manner. You see, Jesus—who was the Son of the living God— laid aside all the glory of His divinity and chose to become a servant for you and me. The Bible says,

> [Jesus] *made Himself of no reputation, taking the form of a bondservant, and coming in the likeness of men. And being found in appearance as a man, He humbled Himself and became obedient to the point of death, even the death of the cross.* (Philippians 2:7–8)

Just before this passage, the apostle Paul wrote, *"Let this mind be in you which was also in Christ Jesus"* (verse 5). That is how a husband is to love his wife. If he loves his wife in this way, that same love will be poured out on his children.

The counsel of the world is the exact opposite. The world tells you to "look out for number one" and to make sure everyone knows who's boss. There is not much love in that kind of an attitude, which is why so many families today are filled with selfishness, anger, jealousy, violence, abuse, unfaithfulness, and divorce—the list could go on. Scripture tells us that those who practice such things cannot inherit God's kingdom. (See 1 Corinthians 6:9–10.)

Being conformed to the image of Christ means being filled with His Holy Spirit. When that happens, you open yourself up to the fruit of the Spirit, which Scripture identifies as *"love, joy, peace, longsuffering, kindness, goodness, faithfulness, gentleness, self-control"* (Galatians 5:22–23).

Husbands, if you will commit, with God's help, to loving your wives as Christ loves each of us, these spiritual qualities will increasingly become integral parts of your character—the character of Jesus Christ in you.

It may not happen overnight, but it will happen. One day, you will find yourself thinking, *Wow, I'm not the same man that I used to be. I'm not responding in anger and impatience to my wife and kids, and I'm not irritable and moody at work anymore!*

That is Christ dwelling within you. That is you being conformed to His image. That is you becoming the person God created you to be.

A Word to Wives

When a husband loves his wife as Christ loved the church, it changes the atmosphere of the home in a dramatic way. The arguments, the disagreements, and the conflicts will decrease; harmony will increase; and the peace that comes with the lordship of Christ will rule. The whole family dynamic will be charged by the glory of God as the husband takes his rightful place as the head of his home, covering his wife and children in prayer, reading the Word with them, and encouraging them in the things of God.

With the husband in his proper role, it becomes much easier for the wife to follow her biblical mandate, which is to willingly and joyfully allow her husband to lead and be the covering for his family. No longer is she forced to take on the duties that her husband has neglected to embrace and fulfill.

Again, I know this flies in the face of a culture focused on liberation, equality in gender roles, and self-fulfillment. But the Bible is clear that to build the kind of family that will survive the long haul and bring glory to God, all the parts must be working correctly. Therefore, the apostle Paul admonished,

> *Wives, submit to your own husbands, as to the Lord. For the husband is head of the wife, as also Christ is head of the church; and He is the Savior of the body. Therefore, just as the church is subject to Christ, so let the wives be to their own husbands in everything.*
>
> (Ephesians 5:22–24)

When a wife submits to her husband, it doesn't mean that she is to become a doormat, and it doesn't mean that she has no say in the home and must remain quiet and obey. Does that describe the biblical relationship between Christ and the church? Is that how you perceive Christ's love for you? It won't if you spend any time reading the Word of God. Our Lord does not deal harshly with us, but tenderly. After all, His desire is for each of us to come to the full stature of a mature believer, standing on His Word and walking in faith. Faith doesn't happen without trust, and trust happens only when you are convinced that the object of trust is committed to doing the best for you.

> **Just as Christ, the Head of the church, is looking out for the best interests of His bride, so, too, the husband, as the head of the home, is constantly looking out for the best interests of his bride.**

That is how marriage must work. Just as Christ, the Head of the church, is looking out for the best interests of His bride, so, too, the husband, as the head of the home, is constantly looking out for the best interests of his bride.

Wives, it matters not whether you are a stay-at-home mom, a checkout clerk at a grocery store, a corporate CEO, a doctor, a lawyer, or any other profession. It doesn't matter if you are in a leadership position in your church. In the home, it is crucial for you to get a Holy Spirit-anointed vision of your husband as the head of your home, the priest who lives to be a covering for you and your children.

A Testimony of Victory

Before we move on, I'd like to share the testimony of a couple in our church who seemed to be in an unredeemable situation. Their story is proof that no one's situation is too far gone when God is involved.

It has often been said that you never know what you have until it's gone and, boy, did we find this famous saying to be so true. In 2001, my wife and I were operating a real estate closing agency, as well as a small used car dealership. We had the perfect life: two beautiful kids, a dream home, and a six-figure income. In 2005, we received a slap in the face from reality. The real estate boom came crashing down to earth and everything from our finances to our marriage was seriously affected. Never in a million years did we expect that our money might run out. As it turned out, we had spent the previous years focusing more on building our own dreams than building God's kingdom first. The stress of our financial woes created a wedge in our marriage, and we slowly started drifting apart. Between bouts of alcohol abuse and infidelity, our marriage was in a state of collapse. Eventually, we lost our home and our businesses.

It was at this time that we decided to move to Florida in hopes that the real estate market would be better than it was in Ohio. We were dead wrong! Again, instead of focusing on God's kingdom, we continued to focus on all the things we no longer had. My wife and I grew bitter and resentful towards each other and decided to separate after thirteen years of marriage.

In my mind, I sort of expected the separation process to be like the ones in the movies: the type in which the husband and wife separate and then, after a couple of weeks apart, go running back in each other's arms once again. Such was not the case for us. We couldn't stand the sight of each other! The only thing that kept us from getting divorced was our lack of money! So, we lived separate lives for two long years.

On Thanksgiving 2009, Erika was in a horrible accident that almost claimed her life. This accident brought things into perspective for both of us. With no friends or family in Florida, we quickly realized that our little family of four was all we had to lean on. We decided to work at saving our marriage. And to do that, we both knew that we would need God back in our lives again.

The Sunday we walked into the Faith Center, we both knew that this was where we needed to be. Bishop Fernandez was teaching a series on having success in your marriage, family, and finances. It was just what we needed to hear. Thanks to this powerful message and the truth found in God's Word, we have now been married for seventeen years and our bond is stronger than it has ever been. We have learned to put God first and foremost in every- and anything that we do in our lives. If anyone is wondering whether or not this message works, I am here to say, "Yes, it does!" This message, through the power of the Holy Spirit, saved our marriage. Words cannot begin to express our gratitude.

How About the Kids?

In a Christian home, children have a crucial role, as well. In Colossians 3:20, Paul counseled, *"Children, obey your parents in all things, for this is well pleasing to the Lord."* God created this world to be filled with harmony and peace, but when sin came on the scene, it shattered that peace, replacing it with rebellion and chaos. But Christ came to set us free from that confusion, and there is no place where that freedom should be demonstrated more than in a home where Christ is Lord.

Today, our culture has given the green light for kids to act out in rebellion against their parents. From music to movies to Internet sites, in school and on the streets, kids are exerting an unholy independence from parental authority at the earliest ages, and that rebellion has led to a tidal wave of negative consequences throughout society.

The Bible is clear on the issue of rebellion. God puts it in the same category as witchcraft.

> *For rebellion is as the sin of witchcraft, and stubbornness is as iniquity and idolatry. Because you have rejected the word of the LORD, He also has rejected you from being king.* (1 Samuel 15:23)

Witchcraft is nothing less than the working out of the same wickedness that caused Satan to be thrown from the halls of heaven, where he wanted to be equal to God.

In God's economy, love and obedience are closely interrelated. Jesus tells us that if we love Him, we will keep His commandments. (See John 14:15.) Moms and dads, if there is one thing that is essential to raising kids who will be able to stand strong in their faith, it is teaching them the importance of obedience. The Bible tells us that *"evil men and impostors will grow worse and worse, deceiving and being deceived"* (2 Timothy 3:13), and the only way Christians will be able to stand against this evil will be through obedience to God.

But you must continue in the things which you have learned and been assured of, knowing from whom you have learned them, and that from childhood you have known the Holy Scriptures, which are able to make you wise for salvation through faith which is in Christ Jesus. (verses 14–15)

> **Honoring your parents—obeying them if they are present in the home and giving them the respect God says they deserve—will prompt God to bless your life, so that your years on the earth are long and fruitful.**

And the best time to learn obedience is in childhood. For children—from the youngest age until they establish their own households—God's line of authority runs through their parents. Children, God wants you to respect and obey your parents. It is also important that you never speak disrespectfully to them—regardless of your relationship (or lack of relationship) with them. Honoring your mother and your father is something that God desires. In fact, doing so actually fulfills one of the Ten Commandments: *"Honor your father and your mother."* (See, for example, Exodus 20:12.) Additionally, it is a commandment that comes with an awesome promise: *"That your days may be long upon the land which the* LORD *your God is giving you"* (verse 12). Honoring your parents—obeying them if they are present in the home and giving them the respect God says they deserve—will prompt God to bless your life, so that your years on the earth are long and fruitful.

> *"Honor your father and mother," which is the first commandment with promise: "that it may be well with you and you may live long on the earth."* (Ephesians 6:2–3)

The Most Important Family

Many individuals—men and women, moms and dads, children young and old—are reading these pages and thinking of the overwhelming problems they face in their own homes and families. There are many Christian wives with ungodly husbands, just as there are godly husbands whose wives are not following Christ. Similarly, there are kids with parents who are almost impossible to honor, obey, and respect.

How does God expect His children to follow His Word in such circumstances? By His grace and through the power of His Holy Spirit. Jesus said, *"In the world you will have tribulation"* (John 16:33) from all sorts of individuals and groups who do not share the faith and love you have in Christ. Some of those individuals will be family members. Our duty and privilege is to model the humility of Christ, even in the midst of persecution. Jesus promised us that, in those situations, we could *"be of good cheer, I have overcome the world"* (verse 33). We will overcome because, through His death and resurrection, Jesus has overcome the world.

The apostle Paul said, *"If it is possible, as much as depends on you, live peaceably with all men"* (Romans 12:18)—with those who are believers and those who are not. We are to bless those who assault us, overcoming evil with good. (See Romans 12:21.) We are to be a light to those individuals who oppose our faith, so that some will actually come to faith in Christ.

Remember, as a child of God, washed in the blood of Jesus Christ, you are a member of the most important family in heaven and earth. It is God's family, and it is founded on perfect love and acceptance. *"Now, therefore, you are no longer strangers and foreigners, but fellow citizens with the saints and members of the household of God"* (Ephesians 2:19). You are no longer strangers, as are those outside of His family. Instead, you stand at the highest order of acceptance, and the persecution you receive from those who are strangers and foreigners to this heavenly family cannot touch or harm you.

In fact, as Paul declared, we can stand in assurance of that truth because *"in all these things we are more than conquerors through Him who loved us"* (Romans 8:37). There is nothing—neither death nor life, neither angels nor demonic forces, neither present hardships nor the specter of tomorrow's troubles—that can separate you from the love of God, your heavenly Father, the Head of your eternal family. (See Romans 8:38–39.)

Part III:

FINANCES

Economy is half the battle of life. It is not so hard to earn money as to spend it well.

—Charles Spurgeon
Best-selling classic author

I will place no value on anything I have or may possess, except in relation to the kingdom of God. If anything will advance the interests of the kingdom, it shall be given away or kept, only as by giving or keeping it I shall most promote the glory of Him to whom I owe all my hopes in time and eternity.

—David Livingstone
Missionary and explorer

Chapter Twelve

What Is True Prosperity?

As God's children, we can rest assured that our heavenly Father cares about every aspect of our lives. In each area in which we are struggling to make sense of our lives, God is there with abundant grace, power, and provision. Perhaps nowhere is this more evident than in the realm of our finances.

I have spent a lot of time over the years studying Scripture to discover what God has to say about living under His blessings of abundance, and I have discovered that He has quite a lot to say—and it is all focused on the benefits derived from being His children. God desires those who are called by His name to prosper and to have all that we need to live fruitful lives on this earth. Whatever is happening around us, no matter the calamities that other people face, God has demonstrated that His children need not struggle to have enough when He has promised to supply all of our needs out of the abundance of His heavenly storehouse.

An Issue of Trust

God wants us, His people, to prosper in all that we set our hands to do. His Word says that when other people fail, His children will succeed. When other people are going down in defeat, His children are to lead lives of victory. When other people don't have enough, His children are to have more than enough. In fact, when times are tough, God wants the church to act as His hands, extended to a world in need. We are to be the ones providing not just spiritual answers but also material responses to the crucial physical needs that other people face.

Many of us have seen this in operation to a limited degree, as churches and other Christian ministries have given food, clothing, finances, and other essential helps to those hurt in the economic downturn our nation has faced. Yet, in too many cases, we are seeing God's people struggling in the same ways that the world around us is struggling. Many Christians are losing their jobs, their homes, their cars, and their bank accounts at the same rate as people who do not know God's power or live under His authority. Too many Christians are having trouble paying their bills. Many men and women who have been walking in faith for years, living in prosperity and abundance as God's children, are now experiencing the same hardships as the world around them. Why is that?

For many of God's children, it comes down to one simple issue: our Father wants us to trust in Him instead of in our riches or circumstances. The unsaved—those who do not know God—have no hope, no inheritance, and no riches other than those that they find here on earth. When their world falls out from under them—when they lose their jobs, when their houses are repossessed, or when all that they have worked for slips out of their grasp in an instant—they have nowhere else to turn than the government or the kindness of charities.

This should not be so with God's people. The psalmist wrote,

God is our refuge and strength, a very present help in trouble. Therefore we will not fear, even though the earth be removed, and though the mountains be carried into the midst of the sea; though its waters roar and be troubled, though the mountains shake with its swelling.
(Psalm 46:1–3)

God is our refuge and strength in every situation, whenever trouble knocks on our doors. As children of God, safely covered by the blood of Jesus Christ, we have no need to fear, even when things around us are falling apart, when the economy is crumbling, and when we don't know where our next dollar is coming from. Even if the earth is removed from its foundation and the mountains slide into the sea, we will not be moved, because God, by the power of His Holy Spirit, is in our midst and will bring us His victory and deliverance in every single situation.

That is the inheritance of the servants of God Almighty. The promise of Psalm 46 is the foundation of all our abundance, our prosperity, our success, and our blessings in this life. And herein lies the problem for so many Christians, and the reason so many are struggling in debt, doubt, and despair. They have lived so long trusting in what they can see—in their jobs, in their bank accounts, in their homes, and in their possessions—instead of trusting God, loving Him, and allowing Him to chart their financial ships. They have let the things of this world become their hope instead of embracing God as their all in all.

Jesus said, *"You cannot serve both God and money"* (Matthew 6:24 NLT). He said that if we love and serve the one, we will hate and reject the other. (See verse 24.) If you are not sure which is more important to you, which one you could do without—Jesus or your financial security—then money has already won the contest. Sadly, it has become your lord, and Christ has been relegated to second place in your life.

In today's culture, many of us have bought into the notion that not only can we love money and God at the same time, but, somehow, a godly character and a blessed lifestyle is found in having more and more material possessions. For years, too many of God's children have blurred the line between His blessings in their lives and their own greed and desire for what this world can give them. Today, many of them are now facing the consequences.

Prosperity is part of the covenant blessing God has for all who will trust Him and make Jesus Christ the Lord of their lives.

I strongly believe that prosperity is part of the covenant blessing God has for all who will trust Him and make Jesus Christ the Lord of their lives. In Deuteronomy 28, God delineates the awesome blessings He promised to pour out over

His chosen people, Israel, if they would listen to Him and obey His commands. I encourage you to take a few minutes to read this incredible chapter because these same blessings are yours through the finished work of Christ. It is a catalog of the absolute abundance that those who trust in God can expect in their lives.

In Galatians, the apostle Paul explained that as blood-bought saints through Jesus Christ, we are heirs of the promises that God gave to Abraham and his descendants.

> *Christ has redeemed us from the curse of the law...that the blessing of Abraham might come upon the Gentiles in Christ Jesus, that we might receive the promise of the Spirit through faith.* (Galatians 3:13–14)

God has promised us access to His many blessings. But these blessings are conditional; they are not automatic for us as God's children. There is a key that opens this door of blessing, and that key is hearing and obeying God's Word.

> *The LORD will open to you His good treasure, the heavens, to give the rain to your land in its season, and to bless all the work of your hand. You shall lend to many nations, but you shall not borrow. And the LORD will make you the head and not the tail; you shall be above only, and not be beneath, if you heed the commandments of the LORD your God, which I command you today, and are careful to observe them.* (Deuteronomy 28:12–13)

The life of the child of God is a life of faith and trust, putting Him above everything and everyone in this life. As we have seen, the condition of living a truly blessed, abundant life is what Jesus identified as the most important commandment in Scripture: *"You shall love the LORD your God with all your heart, with all your soul, with all your mind, and with all your strength"* (Mark 12:30). That is the first prerequisite for receiving all of God's wonderful blessings and promises. And the second commandment is just as important: *"You shall love your neighbor as yourself"* (verse 31).

A Return to Abundance

These two crucial directives from the heart of God are the linchpins from which all our prosperity in this life is based. In America, we who call ourselves "One nation under God" have been living in an economy that has been on the ropes for several years now. I have taken some time to reflect on why even Christians are struggling to make ends meet and how we can get back to a place of true prosperity. I believe the key is this: we need to repent of an attitude that has expected God's blessings without following His plan. Then, we must return to His ways, follow His Word, and stand in faith for the resources we need to live.

And what is the prosperity that He has promised? Here is how the apostle Paul explained it: *"God is able to make all grace abound toward you, that you, always having all sufficiency in all things, may have an abundance for every good work"* (2 Corinthians 9:8). I don't know about you, but the abundance I want and the abundance I need are often two different things. The car I drive, the house I live in, and the clothes I wear might be less than I want, but if I am trusting wholly in God to supply all my needs, according to His riches in glory, then I can rest assured that the abundance He has provided will always be more than equal to the place to which He has called me in this life. In other words, I can do all that He has set before me with the resources He has provided.

> **Too many people are not satisfied with where God has placed them, and so, they push ahead of God's will and timing, borrow money to buy more than they can afford, and, before they know it, are in over their heads.**

The problem is that too many people are not satisfied with where God has placed them, and so, they push ahead of God's will and timing, borrow money to buy more than they can afford, and, before they know it, are in over their heads. Then, they question God's goodness, saying, "Lord, I thought You wanted to prosper me." It's time we learn the difference between God's prosperity and our own presumption.

Presumption is what escalated U.S. consumer debt to an estimated $2.4 trillion at the end of 2010—and this did not include mortgage debt. Presumption is what has caused America to suffer more than 1.5 million personal bankruptcy filings in that same year. Presumption is what has turned America from a nation that lends to a nation that borrows. Presumption is what has turned us from a people who saves and puts money away for a "rainy day" to a people who cannot get our fill of buying the newest things.

Material things are going to pass away. In the long run, our earthly possessions are the sand upon which too many of us have built our hopes, rather than the solid rock of God's unchanging Word. How can we get back to the basics of faith and God's abundance for our lives? I believe there are some clear steps.

Which Would You Rather Have?

There is an old hymn that we used to sing at church entitled "I'd Rather Have Jesus." The first stanza of this profound and moving song goes like this:

I'd rather have Jesus than silver or gold;

I'd rather be His than have riches untold;

I'd rather have Jesus than houses or lands,

I'd rather be led by His nail-pierced hand.[33]

Those words, written many years ago, express the deepest longing of a heart that has been touched by God's mercy through salvation in Jesus Christ. When we come to Christ, when we have tasted of the abundant life He offers, our first inclination is to give up everything and follow Him. He seems to be all we will ever need in this life and in the life to come.

Of course, that is the proper response. Jesus said, *"If anyone desires to come after Me, let him deny himself, and take up his cross, and follow Me"* (Matthew 16:24). That means giving up all self-serving ambitions, all self-made plans for riches and gain, and all secret motivations that run counter to Christ's total lordship in our lives.

Remember the wealthy young ruler who came to Jesus and asked Him what he had to do to inherit eternal life? (See Matthew 19:16–22.) Jesus told the young man that if he wanted eternal life, he needed to keep God's commandments. The young ruler happily told Jesus that he had kept all the commandments from a young age. He asked the Savior, *"What do I still lack?"* (Matthew 19:20). Jesus told him that there was one more thing he had to do:

> *If you want to be perfect, go, sell what you have and give to the poor, and you will have treasure in heaven; and come, follow Me.* (verse 21)

When the rich young ruler heard this, he went away sad because, as Scripture tells us, *"he had great possessions"* (verse 22). While he had an idea that following Christ would fulfill his deep longing for spiritual completeness, he found the cost too great to pay. In the end, his riches meant more to him than his love for Christ.

It's Time for a Reality Check!

So it is with many Christians today. With their mouths, they claim Christ as Lord and Savior, and they have fooled themselves into thinking that Christ is truly their Lord. For many, however, tough economic times have exposed the shallowness of their commitment to Christ. Riches have been their real lord. Now is the time to repent and turn back to God in complete and total trust.

After the rich young ruler left, Jesus exposed one of the greatest obstacles to fruitfulness in God's kingdom:

> *Assuredly, I say to you that it is hard for a rich man to enter the kingdom of heaven. And again I say to you, it is easier for a camel to go through the eye of a needle than*

for a rich man to enter the kingdom of God.
                                        (Matthew 19:23–24)

The world insists that in order to succeed, you must put yourself first and not let anyone or anything get in the way of your success. Yet Jesus said that whoever embraces that attitude will lose everything, while the one who offers up his life in full surrender to loving and serving God will gain the true riches of the kingdom. (See Luke 9:24.) Too many Christians have bought into the world's mentality of "grab all you can" and are now being forced to reevaluate what is of most value in life. It seems as though God has placed many of His children in a situation in which they have no alternative but to surrender all to Him. Their jobs and careers, their 401(k) plans, their homes, their cars—everything they thought was essential to a good life—is now on the line. And God is saying, in effect, "Let it go so that I can fill your life with the true riches of My kingdom."

God is not relegating His children to a lifetime of poverty and lack. That would be counter to His Word. But, in many cases, He may be insisting that our priorities change, that we no longer seek after worldly riches but pursue instead true riches from above.

First Things First

In Matthew 6, Jesus addressed a fundamental issue that underlies our need, as humans, to acquire and increase our possessions. That issue is *fear.* We all have the need to know that we and those we love will have food enough to eat, clothing enough to wear, a roof over our heads, and enough income to meet all the needs that come our way. Those desires are not wrong. In fact, the writer of Proverbs counsels us to consider the simple ant:

Go to the ant, you sluggard! Consider her ways and be wise, which, having no captain, overseer or ruler, provides her supplies in the summer, and gathers her food in the harvest.   (Proverbs 6:6–8)

You might also recall that as the steward of Pharaoh's Egyptian kingdom, Joseph commanded that a supply of grain be stored to counter a coming famine. (See Genesis 41.)

God is not upset by our diligence in working to provide for the needs of our families and loved ones. But there is a difference between godly diligence and human greed. If you have found yourself caught up in the whirlwind of acquiring wealth, and if you find yourself given to building riches and an earthly kingdom, take heed.

Jesus warned,

Do not lay up for yourselves treasures on earth, where moth and rust destroy and where thieves break in and steal; but lay up for yourselves treasures in heaven, where neither moth nor rust destroys and where thieves do not break in and steal. (Matthew 6:19–20)

> **The treasure we lay up in heaven comes to us as we pour out our lives in love and service to God and to others—doing what God has put before us, no matter how insignificant it might seem.**

What are the treasures that we can *"lay up...in heaven"*? They are eternal treasures that come from giving ourselves to loving and worshipping God, spending time with Him, loving and serving others who cannot give to us in return, and sharing the good news of the gospel with those in need. In short, the treasure we lay up in heaven comes to us as we pour out our lives in love and service to God and to others—doing what God has put before us, no matter how insignificant it might seem.

And what about our daily needs? Jesus addressed them, too, saying,

Do not worry about your life, what you will eat or what you will drink; nor about your body, what you will put on. Is not life more than food and the body more than clothing? Look at the birds of the air, for they neither sow

nor reap nor gather into barns; yet your heavenly Father feeds them. Are you not of more value than they?...Why do you worry about clothing? Consider the lilies of the field, how they grow: they neither toil nor spin; and yet I say to you that even Solomon in all his glory was not arrayed like one of these. (Matthew 6:25–26, 28–29)

Giving no thought to acquiring the things of this world truly is a radical idea, seemingly foreign to our earthbound way of thinking. But we serve a radical God who desires to give us all things pertaining to life in His kingdom. (See 2 Peter 1:3.) Following His plan, laid out in His Word, is the only true path to prosperity. God is not telling us to live passive lives in which we patiently wait for His blessings to rain down. Instead, He is inviting us to be about His business on earth, praying and working for His kingdom and will to be established in our realm of influence. As we abandon ourselves to His lordship in all areas, He promises to supply all of our needs out of His unlimited abundance.

Jesus put it this way:

Seek first the kingdom of God and His righteousness, and all these things shall be added to you.
(Matthew 6:33)

Seek True Riches

King David was one individual who learned the matchless value of seeking after the true riches of God's kingdom. As the ruler over an expanding kingdom, he had access to plenty of this world's goods and spent his days living in the lap of luxury. But David considered God his inheritance, and knowing Him to be the treasure he desired. In Psalm 27, David wrote of his only desire:

One thing I have desired of the LORD, that will I seek: that I may dwell in the house of the LORD all the days of my life, to behold the beauty of the LORD, and to inquire in His temple. (verse 4)

Despite all the trappings of being king, David desired only to dwell in the house of the Lord all the days of his life, to bask in God's glory and splendor, and to meditate upon His unsearchable ways.

Because we are children of God through Jesus Christ, our access to the house of the Lord is much easier and more clearly marked than David's was. We have the Holy Spirit to guide us into all truth. We have the unsearchable riches of God's Word to a degree of which David could only dream. For David, the house of the Lord was a tabernacle made by human hands. Today, we have no need to go to a physical building to behold God's glory. *"The Most High does not dwell in temples made with hands"* (Acts 7:48). Instead, He dwells in our hearts through the transforming power of His Holy Spirit. You and I have become God's temple. But the *"one thing"* that drove David's heart has not changed. Knowing God, and being known by Him, is still the one treasure that trumps all others.

This type of devotion and commitment is what God seeks from each of us. This is a picture of seeking first God's kingdom, which, according to Jesus, is the prerequisite for receiving the abundant supply that God promises for all our earthly needs.

A Lifestyle of Love and Devotion

It can be a challenge to maintain the devotion and love that God seeks from each one of us. But I believe that embracing such a life of worship and commitment to Christ is the foundation for receiving the true abundance and prosperity that God wants to pour into us daily. He has no problem prospering those of His children who have died to the things of this world. That is what Paul meant when he wrote,

> *I have been crucified with Christ; it is no longer I who live, but Christ lives in me; and the life which I now live in the flesh I live by faith in the Son of God, who loved me and gave Himself for me.* (Galatians 2:20)

You might think that such a lifestyle of faith and commitment to God is impossible. In the flesh, it certainly is. But, as a Christian, you have the Spirit of God within you, and that is the basis for all transformation in your life. If you will ask God daily to change your heart and mind, to give you the mind of Christ, He will do it. It will come as you spend time in God's Word, in worship, and in prayer, thanking Him for transforming you into the image of Christ.

> **As a Christian, you have the Spirit of God within you, and that is the basis for all transformation in your life.**

As that happens, and as the things of this world take a backseat to the things of God, you will be amazed at how your circumstances change as God pours into your life not just the riches of His kingdom but also more and more of the resources of this earth.

Chapter Thirteen

Dealing with Debt

John and Diane represent many young American couples today who are working hard to build their version of the American dream. They've been happily married for six years, have two preschool-aged children, and recently purchased their own home, a three-bedroom ranch in the suburbs, far enough away from the chaos, crime, and crowds of the city but close enough for John to commute downtown for work each day.

John has a stable job doing marketing for a major manufacturing firm, but his salary isn't quite large enough for his family to live on comfortably. So, Diane also works part-time at a local retailer to help make ends meet. Even with Diane's additional income, they still struggle to afford the extras, such as summer vacations, Christmas and birthday presents for the kids, and a weekly night out as a couple. A year and a half ago, they began to put some of their discretionary spending on a couple of credit cards, which they fully intended to pay off on a monthly basis.

Things seemed to go smoothly for the first few months, but it wasn't long before pressure mounted as car payments, mortgage payments, utility bills, along with a barrage of unforeseen expenses, began to eat away at the couple's monthly budget. When money was tight, credit cards increasingly became their go-to safety valve to purchase groceries and gas or to buy that thing they "couldn't do without."

After a year of living in this fashion, their spending caused them to fall further and further behind on their monthly expenses and credit card bills. Letters and phone calls from collectors took an unnerving toll on the couple's happiness. Eventually, John and Diane were forced to make some tough decisions about their lifestyle and future.

Debt is the worst poverty.   —Thomas Fuller

An Attitude of Entitlement

Does John and Diane's story sound familiar to you? Sadly, millions of Americans have fallen into a similar trap, convinced that easy credit and a "buy now, pay later" attitude is the American way. Far too many Americans have lost sight of the commitment to strong financial stewardship that previous generations embraced as crucial to their survival. In fact, today, our nation is saddled with debt—both public and private—of a magnitude unimaginable to previous generations, and the reason has much to do with the attitude of entitlement that has established itself within our nation's psyche.

Take, for instance, the national debt—the sum of all outstanding debt owed by the federal government. When President Barack Obama took office on January 20, 2009, America's national debt was an astounding $10.6 trillion! By the end of his first term, that figure is projected to be around $16.5 trillion.[34] As of this writing, the current debt figure is more than $14 trillion, or more than $46,000 for every American citizen!

Such an ocean of debt has come from years of spending on programs and projects that America's forefathers never conceived of, many of which the government had no constitutional authority to create. In 2010, the U.S. government spent $1.34 trillion more than it took in. The 2011 budget deficit is projected to be close to $1.5 trillion.[35]

On a personal level, the financial situation of the average American has never been worse. In 2010, the total amount of U.S. consumer debt—which includes credit cards and other debt but not mortgages or home equity loans—stood at $2.4 trillion. In 1982, the average American worker saved more than 11 percent of his or her discretionary income. By 2008, that personal savings rate had plummeted to 0.4 percent. Many economists blame this decline on years of easy credit that sucked Americans into a nonstop buying spree, which has been checked only by our nation's struggling economy. Thankfully, in 2010, Americans raised their average savings rate back up to 5.3 percent of their annual incomes.

It is not a stretch to suggest that an attitude of personal entitlement has been the foundation for much of what has gone wrong with both our public and private finances in America. In the 1960s, public initiatives were created in order to battle poverty and urban blight. Over the past forty-five years, these social programs have exploded into publicly funded monstrosities that have conditioned millions of Americans to expect the government to be their cradle-to-grave caretaker. What began as billions of dollars set aside to help the poor, the unemployed, the orphaned, and the needy has morphed into a boondoggle of trillions of taxpayer dollars going into the hands of an ever-growing army of "needy" individuals.

> **The idea of delayed gratification—that one should save and have the money in hand before making a purchase—has become a foreign idea to many.**

As for our personal spending habits, untold millions of Americans have grown up with an attitude that there should be no limits put on their happiness and comfort, and that they should be able to purchase whatever their hearts desire. The idea of delayed gratification—that one should save and have the money in hand before making a purchase—has become a foreign idea to many. Instead, attitudes have taken root that insist only the newest and best will do, bigger is always better, and we must have it now.

Never spend your money before you have earned it.
—Thomas Jefferson

Finding Contentment

How foreign the "have it all now" sentiment is to the gospel of Jesus Christ, who, Scripture tells us, *"being in the form of God, did not consider it robbery to be equal with God, but made Himself of no reputation, taking the form of a bondservant, and coming in the likeness of men"* (Philippians 2:6–7). This same mind-set—that of a servant—is to be in us, as well, motivating and informing all we are and all we do. Think about it! A servant committed to his master is not thinking about getting more and more. His or her thoughts are centered on giving and serving.

In today's culture, however, self is king, even among God's people. Too many of us have bought into the "kingdom of me," a mentality that allows our appetites and urges to control our every behavior. The price many of us have paid is horrendous. America is drowning in an ocean of debt. We need to reverse our direction.

Such a reversal is possible if we will reach out and take it. It begins when we understand that true prosperity starts with contentment. While the Bible is filled with God's promises to prosper and bless those who trust in Him, the apostle Paul wrote, *"Now godliness with contentment is great gain. For we brought nothing into this world, and it is certain we can carry nothing out"* (1 Timothy 6:6–7). As long as God provides us with the necessities of life—which He has promised to do in abundance—we can have great contentment in life.

> *Let your conduct be without covetousness; be content with such things as you have. For He Himself has said, "I will never leave you nor forsake you."* (Hebrews 13:5)

You see, if we embrace an attitude of contentment, God becomes our inheritance, both in this life and in the next. He desires to be of far greater value to us than any earthly possession.

Paul cautioned that those who seek after wealth will inevitably fall into temptations and become trapped.

> *But those who desire to be rich fall into temptation and a snare, and into many foolish and harmful lusts which*

drown men in destruction and perdition.
(1 Timothy 6:9)

I believe that the financial duress many individuals and families face on a daily basis is part of what Paul warned us about. Striving after riches has plunged many into a downward spiral of financial pain and heartache, and only God's power and mercy can save them.

I will never leave you nor forsake you.   (Hebrews 13:5)

Digging Out and Standing Tall

Becoming buried in debt doesn't happen overnight for most people, and digging out won't happen that quickly, either. But I believe that God has a special grace for those who find themselves in this particular kind of bondage, and that grace can lead even the most hopelessly bound individual into financial freedom and true prosperity.

This book isn't meant to provide detailed advice on how to consolidate debt, work with creditors, establish a budget, and get back on firm financial footing. There is an abundance of books, Web sites, and organizations that can provide detailed instructions for paying off debt and achieving financial freedom. Nevertheless, I believe I *can* provide you with some basic counsel on embracing a lifestyle of godly contentment that will help you to be a wise steward of the resources with which God has blessed you. .

With the promises of God in your heart and on your lips, you can declare, *"I can do all things through Christ who strengthens me"* (Philippians 4:13). You can say to yourself, *"My God shall supply all* [my needs] *according to His riches in glory by Christ Jesus"* (verse 19).

It Takes Determination

When you are determined that nothing will hold you back from all that God has for your life, you will be on the way to absolute financial freedom. I want to encourage you to make the following steps your battle cries for freedom, and I want you to declare them daily in thought, word, and deed.

Step 1: Determine to Live within God's Standard of Blessing

I believe that God has a standard of living that we should work to meet. The standard isn't the same for everyone. We each need to pray, seeking God's guidance, and find that place of perfect abundance that He has for us. Problems arise when we compare ourselves with others, live above our means, get in over our heads, and try to swim in waters God never meant for us.

Despite what you may have been told, God has not destined all of His children to be millionaires. Not everyone is meant to live in a mansion, drive a luxury car, and make multimillion-dollar business deals. Not everyone has the aptitude and spiritual anointing to be the steward of a large fortune. God has given that grace to some individuals, and their responsibility is to live humble, holy lives as servants of God. Their wealth was not given to them to fulfill fleshly lusts and desires but to fulfill God's destiny for their lives.

> **God has promised to make His grace abound in your circumstances so that you will always have sufficient provision for that to which He has called you.**

Other individuals have different callings that don't include great amounts of wealth. Their obligation, before God and their fellow man, is to follow the path upon which God has placed them, with the full assurance that His grace is sufficient for that path. (See 2 Corinthians 12:9.)

Rest assured, God has promised to make His grace abound in your circumstances so that you will always have sufficient provision for that to which He has called you. (See 2 Corinthians 9:8.) As God's children, we can repeat the words of the apostle Paul: *"I have learned in whatever state I am, to be content"* (Philippians 4:11).

Step 2: Determine to Be Thankful

One of the chief issues that God had to deal with in the nation of Israel was their grumbling and murmuring. God had set them apart from all other peoples on the earth, raising them up to be the physical demonstration of His mercy and faithfulness to the rest of the world. The only thing He asked them to do was to trust Him implicitly, and He promised to bless them above all other peoples on the earth.

But, as He led them through the wilderness and into the inheritance He desired to give them, over and over, they complained about their circumstances, His provision, and the difficulties they faced. In one instance, the children of Israel grew so discouraged that they began complaining against God and His servant Moses for leading them out of bondage in Egypt and into the wilderness. They complained about the lack of food and water, even though God had abundantly supplied their every need. As they complained, fiery serpents came out of the wilderness, biting and killing many of them. Their own attitudes had gotten them into trouble; they had replaced faith and thankfulness with a spirit of murmuring and rebellion. Even in their sinfulness, however, God was there with the answer: a serpent on a pole, which the people had only to look at in order to be healed from the deadly serpent bites. (See Numbers 21:5–9.)

The apostle Paul told us that scriptural examples such as this were given for our benefit, so that we could know how God wants us to respond when troubles come. (See 1 Corinthians 10:1–13.) The Bible is clear that if we will maintain a thankful heart before God, regardless of our circumstances, we will be strengthened for victory in every trial we face.

> *Rejoice always, pray without ceasing, in everything give thanks; for this is the will of God in Christ Jesus for you.* (1 Thessalonians 5:16–18)

Are you having a problem paying your bills? Give thanks to God that, through Christ, your needs will be met. Have you been laid off from your job? Give thanks to God for having another, better source of income waiting for you. Many people today are under tremendous stress as they face financial uncertainty. There is only one answer: as difficult as your circumstances are, give thanks to God for His unending care for you.

Rest assured that maintaining a thankful heart to God is not an exercise in futility. Rather, it is an intentional determination that, no matter what comes your way, you will look expectantly to God for the answer.

Step 3: Determine Not to Fear

More than any other emotion, fear seems to have taken center stage in the hearts of men and women across our nation. For individuals who have lived for so long with little or no concern about the things of tomorrow, to suddenly have financial certainty pulled out from under them is a devastating blow. But that is exactly what is happening today. For many, their foundation has crumbled before their very eyes, leaving them with nothing to hold on to.

But for those who know God, this is a time for trust. God is telling us:

> *Don't be afraid, for I am with you. Don't be discouraged, for I am your God. I will strengthen you and help you. I will hold you up with my victorious right hand.*
> (Isaiah 41:10 NLT)

Remember, *"God has not given us a spirit of fear, but of power and of love and of a sound mind"* (2 Timothy 1:7). Knowing that He will supply all your needs out of His storehouse of abundance, you can boldly declare, "I will not fear."

Step 4: Determine to Trust God for Financial Freedom

Walking in the level of prosperity God has promised boils down to trusting Him to accomplish His perfect will in all that concerns you. As you feed daily on God's Word, meditating on

Walking in the level of prosperity God has promised boils down to trusting Him to accomplish His perfect will in all that concerns you.

the riches of His glory and mercy, you will find your circumstances lining up with His will to an ever greater degree. You will find yourself declaring with King David, *"The Lord will perfect that which concerns me"* (Psalm 138:8). Even though you find yourself walking through various trials that test your faith, you will not be moved. Like Job, you will declare that God *"knows the way that I take; when He has tested me, I shall come forth as gold"* (Job 23:10).

Here is the testimony of Natasha, a woman who never wavered in her trust in God, even when her world was in danger of crumbling around her.

I have believed in tithing all my life. From a young age, I was taught to have faith in God, no matter the circumstances. For me, tithing has been such a big part of that faith. Whenever I have failed to tithe, I immediately felt out of sorts, as if something was missing. Through the years, God has proven Himself faithful time and time again. I have never been in financial need; I have never had to ask another person for financial help.

In 2006, after years of searching, God finally blessed me with a home that I could afford to buy. Like many homebuyers at the time, I obtained an interest-only loan that was to become an adjustable-rate loan after three years. In 2008, my real estate agent urged me to consider having the loan modified to a fixed-rate mortgage. She was afraid that the rate would be adjusted to an amount that I wouldn't be able to afford. She introduced me to a man who helped me to fill out the application. This led to several months of back-and-forth dealings with the mortgage company. During this time, my business began to lag and, for the first time, it dawned on me that I could lose my home if the modification was not approved. Nevertheless, I kept praying to God and never lost a night's sleep.

Six months into the process, the bank finally approved the loan modification. My interest rate went from 6.75 percent down to 3.8 *percent. My mortgage payment went from more than $1,000 down to only $533. In addition to that, the bank wrote off more than $20,000 of the loan amount because the house had decreased in value.*

Two years later, in 2010, I received a letter telling me that my account was in default and that I owed more than $23,000, which was due in one month or else the bank would declare me in default. This did not make sense since my mortgage payment had been automatically withdrawn from my checking account each month. After contacting them, I was told that my loan modification had mistakenly put me back into an interest-only loan. None of my payments had been put toward the principal amount of the loan.

I was devastated. After calling my mother, however, I recalled all the teachings on faith I had heard from Pastor Fernandez for so many years. I realized that this was just another mountain for God to move. I said, "Mom, this is going to work out in my favor; you watch." God had blessed me with that house, and I had never gone back on the financial terms. I was sure that He was not about to take it away from me.

Sure enough, before long, I was told that the error had been corrected and that $79,000 had been applied toward the principal amount of my loan. In doing so, my monthly payment was reduced by another one hundred dollars.

There are so many stories of blessing connected to this house that I know God meant for me to have it. I waited a long time to be able to buy it, and God has continuously rewarded me for my patience. Every day, I am learning to trust Him for everything. Every day, I aim to walk in faith, uncompromised.

Going for the Gold

Friend, there is no prosperity God can give you that is more valuable than the eternal truth of Job 23:10. As I have stated throughout this book, becoming like Christ in every way—being conformed to His image—is the greatest goal we can have in this life. Proverbs 4:18 says, *"The path of the just is like the shining sun, that shines ever brighter unto the perfect day."* Every day, as we walk close to God and seek His face, He promises to change us *"from glory to glory"* (2 Corinthians 3:18) into the likeness of His Son.

True prosperity and abundance begins, and ends, with seeing this come to pass in your life and in the lives of your loved ones. My prayer for you is that you will truly "go for the gold," seeking with all your heart to become the person God has created you to be and settling for nothing less than His best in every aspect of your walk on this earth.

Chapter Fourteen

Grace for Giving

Jesus said, *"It is more blessed to give than to receive"* (Acts 20:35), and He showed us how by giving His all—His very life and being—so that we could be reconciled to God. Few Christians today seem to understand that their life in Christ ought to be centered on giving, not getting. While we come to Christ with a life weighed down by cares—seeking cleansing from sin, healing of our bodies, peace for our souls, deliverance from bondage, sanctification of our lives, and the meeting of our daily needs—when we make Jesus our Lord, we place ourselves in the flow of God's unending abundance. Because He has assured us that He will meet all of our needs according to His riches in glory (see Philippians 4:19), we have the liberty to abandon our own agendas and desires and to focus on being vessels for meeting the needs of others.

That's why Jesus told the rich young ruler that he needed to do one more thing in addition to successfully keeping all of God's commandments: *"Sell all that you have and distribute to the poor, and you will have treasure in heaven; and come, follow Me"* (Luke 18:22). Likewise, Jesus clearly tells each of us that in order to truly be His follower...

> *You must turn from your selfish ways, take up your cross, and follow me. If you try to hang on to your life, you will lose it. But if you give up your life for my sake, you will save it. And what do you benefit if you gain the whole world but lose your own soul? Is anything worth more than your soul?* (Matthew 16:24–26 NLT)

Somehow, such an admonition gets lost in our focus on try-ing to making God into our "personal blessings facilitator." We often declare all the Scriptures that say He is going to bless us while ignoring the larger necessity of completely abandoning ourselves—all we are and all we have—to His lordship.

The true grace of God flowing in and through our lives is tied to our willingness to allow Him to make us into graceful and joyful givers, and nowhere is that more clearly demonstrat-ed than in the area of our finances.

Cheerful, Generous Giving

I once heard a story about the wealthy American automak-er Henry Ford, who was approached about donating money for a new hospital in a particular community. Ford made what he considered to be a generous donation of five thousand dollars but was aghast when he read the headlines in the newspaper the next day: "Henry Ford Donates $50,000 to New Hospital." Ford immediately phoned the paper's editor to inform him that there had been a huge mistake, to which the editor replied that he would gladly print a correction: "Henry Ford Reduces Dona-tion to $5,000." The media-savvy carmaker realized that such a twist in the reporting would make him look like a cheapskate, so, he begrudgingly agreed to donate the full $50,000—still, hardly much of a sacrifice for him.

How many times has God placed us in a position to give graciously and cheerfully out of the abundance He has supplied in our lives, only to observe us giving reluctantly, cautiously, or even begrudgingly? Second Corinthians 9 offers a crystal clear view of just how God wants to see His children give, and how He will respond to the attitude that inspires our giving. The apostle Paul compared the giving of our resources—our wise and godly financial stewardship—to a farmer planting seeds in his field, telling us, *"A farmer who plants only a few seeds will get a small crop. But the one who plants generously will get a generous crop"* (verse 6 NLT). Then, Paul said, *"You must each decide in your heart how much to give. And don't give reluctantly or in response to pressure. 'For God loves a person who gives cheerfully'"* (verse 7 NLT).

What is God's response to that which we willingly offer as a gift? He *"will generously provide all you need. Then you will always have everything you need and plenty left over to share with others"* (2 Corinthians 9:8 NLT). You see, we can give with the full assurance that our heavenly Father will never leave us without all that we need—and so much more—for the circumstances in which He has placed us.

> If you give what you do not need, it isn't giving.
>
> —Mother Teresa

Model God's Heart in Giving

There is a story in the book of Mark that powerfully illustrates the attitude God wants us to have as givers. As Jesus sat in the temple one day, He observed people coming to put their offerings into the temple treasury. Many of those who dropped money into the collection box were wealthy, and their offerings were substantial. Then, along came a poor widow, a woman who obviously had little in the way of worldly wealth. As Jesus watched, this widow deposited two small coins—a tiny amount compared to the contributions of the wealthy folks. Yet, as He commented on this woman's actions, Jesus' words revealed the heart of the Father:

> *I tell you the truth, this poor widow has given more than all the others who are making contributions. For they gave a tiny part of their surplus, but she, poor as she is, has given everything she had to live on.*
>
> (Mark 12:43–44 NLT)

How much does God want us to give? Christian author C. S. Lewis observed, "I do not believe one can settle how much we ought to give. I am afraid the only safe rule is to give more than we can spare."[36] That is the heart of God. When He gave His only Son for us, He gave until it hurt. Giving His most precious Son was more than He wanted to spare, yet He gave willingly for you and for me. How can we do any less?

The best part about giving is that our Father has promised to multiply back to us all we have given, so that we will have more than enough for our needs and the needs of those to whom God has called us to minister.

Jesus made this point clearly when He declared,

Give, and you will receive. Your gift will return to you in full—pressed down, shaken together to make room for more, running over, and poured into your lap. The amount you give will determine the amount you get back.   (Luke 6:38 NLT)

What I spent, is gone; what I kept, I lost; but what I gave away will be mine forever.   —Ethel Percy Andrus

Give out of Your Need

The problem with many people today is that, in the realm of giving, they have settled into their comfort zones, giving what is convenient rather than giving, like the widow in the temple, out of their need. They give only out of what remains after the bills have been paid and the week's groceries have been bought instead of giving first into the kingdom, allowing God to make up for any lack.

In 1 Kings, God gave us an example of what happens when we give to Him out of our need. The prophet Elijah was directed by God to go to the village of Zarephath to seek out a widow whom God would use to sustain him with what he needed to live. When he got to the village, sure enough, there was such a woman, to whom Elijah said,

"Please bring me a little water in a cup, that I may drink." And as she was going to get it, he called to her and said, "Please bring me a morsel of bread in your hand."
                                           (1 Kings 17:10–11)

But there was a problem. The woman and her young son were beyond needy, to the point of near starvation. The woman responded,

> As the Lord your God lives, I do not have bread, only a handful of flour in a bin, and a little oil in a jar; and see, I am gathering a couple of sticks that I may go in and prepare it for myself and my son, that we may eat it, and die. (1 Kings 17:12)

The faith of this woman was about to be tested as Elijah, by the prompting of the Holy Spirit, responded to her need.

> Do not fear; go and do as you have said, but make me a small cake from it first, and bring it to me; and afterward make some for yourself and your son. (verse 13)

But Elijah didn't stop there. He made this promise to the woman for her faithfulness in giving to God in the midst of her need:

> For thus says the Lord God of Israel: "The bin of flour shall not be used up, nor shall the jar of oil run dry, until the day the Lord sends rain on the earth." (verse 14)

Scripture relates that because of this woman's faithfulness and obedience to God,

> she went away and did according to the word of Elijah; and she and he and her household ate for many days. The bin of flour was not used up, nor did the jar of oil run dry, according to the word of the Lord which He spoke by Elijah. (verses 15–16)

Follow the Principle of Firstfruits

There is an important scriptural principle in this story: it matters not what is happening around you, the hardships the world is facing, or how bad the economy might be. If you are a child of God, living in the overflow of His abundance and trusting in His care, you can rest assured that your flour and oil will never be depleted. You will always have enough—more than enough—to meet your needs and to succeed in fulfilling God's call on your life. But there is a stipulation. You must be willing to give out of your need, not just your excess. You may not be facing the same dire straits as the widow of Zarephath, and you may not be down to your last two cents, like the widow Jesus observed in the temple, but then again, who is to say what hardships and trials you and I may face down the road? Whatever your circumstances, God wants you to be willing to give to His kingdom first, and then to trust Him to more than meet your every need.

> *Honor the LORD with your possessions, and with the first-fruits of all your increase; so your barns will be filled with plenty, and your vats will overflow with new wine.*
> (Proverbs 3:9–10)

You may not be a farmer with crops and a barn, but the principle remains the same: if you honor God by giving Him the *"firstfruits"* of all you earn, He will make sure that you have an overabundance of everything you need.

God Will Open the Windows of Heaven

God's desire is to *"open for you the windows of heaven and pour out for you such blessing that there will not be room enough to receive it"* (Malachi 3:10). But it is important for you to make sure that your heart is in the right place so that you can receive His blessings of provision.

Take a look at the children of Israel who had returned to Jerusalem following Israel's generations-long exile in Babylon. God had brought His people back and promised to bless them as they trusted and worshipped Him. But, while they started out strong and faithful, it wasn't long before their commitment waned and they began to withhold the firstfruits of their increase from Him. God spoke to them about this through the prophet Malachi, warning them that by holding back both their tithe—the first tenth of their income—and their offerings—voluntary gifts over and above the tithe—they were both robbing Him and bringing a curse of lack upon themselves.

> *Will a man rob God? Yet you have robbed Me! But you say, "In what way have we robbed You?" In tithes and offerings. You are cursed with a curse, for you have robbed Me, even this whole nation.* (Malachi 3:8–9)

Look at your own circumstances. Are you guilty of holding back from God the first part of your income? Do you find yourself being stingy toward your heavenly Father when it comes to freewill offerings? If so, this may be the reason why you never seem to have enough money to meet your own needs. Remember, God owns all you have in the first place, and when you give to Him, you are merely giving back what is already His. And God will never allow you to give more than He gives back.

> **Remember, God owns all you have in the first place, and when you give to Him, you are merely giving back what is already His. And God will never allow you to give more than He gives back.**

There is a surefire remedy to this lack—to the curse of poverty that may be hanging over your life. It is the same remedy that God gave to the children of Israel.

> *"Bring all the tithes into the storehouse, that there may be food in My house, and try Me now in this," says the LORD of hosts, "if I will not open for you the windows of heaven and pour out for you such blessing that there will not be room enough to receive it. And I will rebuke the devourer for your sakes, so that he will not destroy the fruit of your ground, nor shall the vine fail to bear fruit for you in the field," says the LORD of hosts; "and all nations will call you blessed, for you will be a delightful land," says the LORD of hosts.* (Malachi 3:10–12)

God's Progression for Your Prosperity

As I read the above passage, I see a clear progression of God's blessing on His people as they obey Him and put His kingdom purposes before their own needs and desires.

1. You bring the tithes and offerings to God.

The first step is yours. The first tenth of all you earn belongs to God and goes to your church or fellowship—the place where you are being fed spiritually, where you are held accountable, and where God has placed you to minister and to be ministered to. Beyond that, God desires that you give offerings from a heart of thankfulness and compassion, as well as a burden to see His kingdom come and His will be done in the earth. Is there a ministry God has placed on your heart that could use your financial partnership? God wants you to give to provide for that need. Is there a television ministry that has blessed you in a time of need? Send an offering that will help them continue the work to which God has called them. Have you noticed a needy family or group in your neighborhood or community that would benefit from a financial gift? You probably don't even need to pray about it. Just step out and help meet the need.

2. God will open the windows of heaven and pour out a blessing larger than you will be able to receive.

The next step is God's, and one that He has already promised to take on your behalf. As you step out in faith and obedience, He will respond with a well-placed blessing at your specific point of need.

3. God will rebuke the devourer, preventing the enemy from destroying the fruit of your labors.

Jesus said that Satan came to kill, steal, and destroy all that pertains to you. He is the devourer. But Jesus came to give you life in abundance, filled to overflowing. (See John 10:10.) When Jesus died on the cross and rose victoriously over the grave, He was openly rebuking the devourer, once and for all, for your sake. Through Jesus, you stand victorious against all the schemes the devil may use to thwart your success and prevent you from receiving the blessings God has promised. You may have to stand strong against the enemy's attacks, but rest assured that as you stand upon God's Word, boldly declaring it in the face of your need, you will see victory in your finances.

4. Everyone around you will know that you are blessed by God.

Instead of being the tail, you will be the head. (See Deuteronomy 28:13.) Instead of having a reputation of poverty and lack, you will be known as the one whom God has blessed.

I never get tired of hearing men and women share how massively God has blessed them after they gave of their resources to His kingdom, trusting their heavenly Father to provide for all their needs.

Although perhaps not always the finest example of Christian charity, the powerful American industrialist John D. Rockefeller was known to have said, "I never would have been able to tithe the first million dollars I ever made if I had not tithed my first salary, which was $1.50 per week."[37] This wealthy gentleman did not start out on top but at the bottom. He first obeyed the smaller things before God raised him to a higher level.

Scripture counsels us not to despise the day of *"small beginnings"* (Zechariah 4:10 NLT)—those seemingly insignificant areas in life that don't add up to much on their own. God will use humble beginnings to test and discipline us for future greatness. How many successful individuals began by sweeping the floors in their company or by serving as an assistant to someone else? God destined them for bigger things, but the path to the top started with *"small beginnings."*

Be a Role Model of Generosity

So it will be with you. You are destined for great things, but those great things may be disguised as small beginnings. As

> **As you are faithful, you will rise, and people around you will witness God's faithfulness to you.**

you are faithful, you will rise, and people around you will witness God's faithfulness to you.

How would you like to serve as a role model for others, who see the results of your giving into God's kingdom? How would you like to be a catalyst for someone else to give out of poverty and lack, all because he or she saw how faithfully you applied God's principles, putting His kingdom before your needs?

All it takes is deciding to start right where you are today. I am convinced that as you give out of your need, God will turn your lack into an abundant harvest so that you will be empowered to become a blessing to others. Your giving will become a cycle of prosperity so that every time you give as unto the Lord, it will come back to you, *"good measure, pressed down, shaken together, and running over"* (Luke 6:38).

Some say that you should never give with the motive of getting something in return. When it comes to giving to God, however, I heartily disagree. If God has promised to *"rebuke the devourer"* (Malachi 3:11) when you are faithful with your tithes and offerings, and if He has promised that when you give into His kingdom, He will give back in such a manner that you will not be able to handle the blessings, then you need to pay attention to those promises.

God will never be a debtor to any human—He never has and never will. When you give in faith, believing His promises and keeping your eyes focused on Christ as your *"exceedingly great reward"* (Genesis 15:1), just like Abraham, God will also prove faithful to you. All around, you will see that your bold faith in God has made the difference. Your life will become a testimony of God's righteousness and faithfulness toward the creation He so loves. And that will be a life well-lived.

Conclusion

Your Hope and Destiny Are Now!

We are living in exciting times. As Christians, even with the uncertainties swirling around us, we do not walk as those who have no hope. Christ Himself has promised that in every circumstance, He will never leave or forsake us. Therefore, we do not have to fear. (See Hebrews 13:5–6.) In fact, we can boldly declare that *"we are more than conquerors through Him who loved us"* (Romans 8:37).

This is God's Word, and it is not to be taken lightly! Our Lord and Savior, Jesus Christ, won the victory over our adversary, the devil. Now, we sit together with Him in the heavenly places of victory and abundance. There is nothing left to be done. As Jesus hung on the cross for our salvation and deliverance, He declared, *"It is finished!"* (John 19:30). Just as Abraham was blessed by God, who established a covenant with him and his descendants forever, we have access to the same blessings of abundance and victory.

Coming into Agreement

In your faith, your family, and your finances, you are standing on the rock-solid foundation of Christ's finished work. In these three areas, no one should stand more confident of success and victory than God's people. Our enemy knows that these are three primary areas of our lives in which conflicts and challenges will occur. Satan's goal is to convince us that we are not victorious, that things are not okay, and that catastrophe and failure are just around the corner. We should never be surprised by these attacks because we are dealing with the master deceiver and the father of lies. (See John 8:44.)

But we also must know how to successfully destroy these attacks and remember that success comes through the power of agreement. My simple question is this: with whom will you come into agreement? Whose report will you believe? For too long, God's people have believed the lies of the devil—that their faith is not strong enough, that their families are too far gone, and that their financial bondage runs too deep for victory to occur. Is that really what God's Word says? Are your problems, your issues, and your needs more powerful than the blood of Jesus? Are your problems the lord of your life, or must they bow their knees to the name that is above every name?

> **You have the power and authority, as God's child, to come into agreement with everything that He says about you in His Word.**

I think you already know the answers to these questions. The blood and the name of the Lord Jesus Christ are the most powerful forces on earth—more powerful in your life than any obstacle set before you! You have the power and authority, as God's child, to come into agreement with everything that He says about you in His Word. You can make the following biblically based declarations over your faith, your family, and your finances:

"I can do all things through Christ who gives me strength for success and victory." (See Philippians 4:13.)

"I commit my ways to the Lord with the confidence that He will establish all my plans." (See Proverbs 16:3 AMP, NLT)

"God has blessed me with every spiritual blessing in the heavenly places in Christ, my Savior and Lord." (See Ephesians 1:3.)

"Because I am born of God through Jesus Christ, I am an overcomer through faith." (See 1 John 5:5.)

These are just a handful of declarations from Scripture that will help you live in victory and authority. I encourage you to dig into the Word on a daily basis to find those hidden treasures of God's truth that will empower you to walk in freedom and discover the destiny for which God created you.

Binding and Loosing

In Matthew 18, Jesus offered a clear picture of the authority we have in Him, an authority that stretches throughout the earth and resounds in the halls of heaven:

> *Assuredly, I say to you, whatever you bind on earth will be bound in heaven, and whatever you loose on earth will be loosed in heaven.*   (Matthew 18:18)

As a child of God, you have the authority of Christ on this earth. The words He speaks, you can speak. The power of the heavenly kingdom is yours. What you do with that power and authority, however, is completely up to you. In your faith, in your family, and in your finances, you have the authority to both bind and loosen.

How do you want to use this authority? The Bible says that death and life reside in the power of your tongue. (See Proverbs 18:21.) Quite simply, your life will reflect what you have been conditioned to speak, day in and day out. To speak life means speaking God's truth. To speak death means speaking, or coming into agreement with, the lies of the devil.

What would happen if you conditioned yourself to always speak God's truth over your faith, your family, and your finances? The enemy would be bound, and God's will would be loosed, in every situation in which you have influence. Where there once was fear, there would be boldness. Where there once was doubt, there would be an incredible assurance that what God has promised, He will perform.

As a child of God, you have the authority to loosen your family members so that they can experience His plan. Likewise,

> **God has a perfect plan for each member of your household, and your words of affirmation, your prayers of faith, and your declarations of His will in their lives hold great sway.**

you have the authority to bind each family member to God's perfect will for his or her life. God has a perfect plan for each member of your household, and your words of affirmation, your prayers of faith, and your declarations of His will in their lives hold great sway.

Similarly, you have the power to either bind or loosen God's financial blessings into your life and the lives of others. Jesus said that with the same measure you give, it will be given back to you. (See Luke 6:38.) Accordingly, the apostle Paul counseled, *"He who sows sparingly will also reap sparingly, and he who sows bountifully will also reap bountifully"* (2 Corinthians 9:6).

Your words are not the only things that can bind and loosen; your actions can, as well. Just as doubt and fear—demonstrated through your words, attitudes, and actions—can hold back God's blessings, putting your faith into action will produce a harvest of God's richest blessings.

Where Two or Three Agree

In Matthew 18:19, Jesus made clear to us the power we have when we agree in prayer:

> *Again I say to you that if two of you agree on earth concerning anything that they ask, it will be done for them by My Father in heaven.*

I encourage you to find one or two trustworthy individuals who will agree with you in prayer for the answers you desire. Make a covenant with them to pray and believe, standing on the Word of God, until the answers come. If you need an increase of faith, ask for it, and God will supply it. If you need healing in your family, agree with those prayer partners, and it will come. If you need deliverance or a miracle in your finances, agree in prayer, for He has promised to open a window of abundance over your life to the extent that you will not have room enough to receive it.

You and I make a majority before God. Thus, there is no better time than now for us to agree. I would like to close this book with a simple prayer of agreement that in the coming months and years, God will do great things in your faith walk, in your family, and in your finances. Let's agree together in prayer:

Father in heaven, You have promised to bless those who love You by giving them the desires of their hearts. Today, I come into agreement with my dear friends that You will increase their faith in a powerful way, anointing them to believe for great things in their unique realms of influence.

I speak health, healing, and wholeness over every family relationship, and I ask that You would mend every brokenness and conflict that exists, bringing *"the unity of the Spirit in the bond of peace"* (Ephesians 4:3) into every corner of their families' lives.

Finally, Father, I pray Your abundant blessings over their finances and ask that You would bring them increase in creative and unusual ways. Open opportunities, give them great favor with those who can bring them increase, and pour out a blessing into their lives that will be more than enough for those You have called them to help and support. Let the days and years ahead be times of abundant fruitfulness as they seek to do Your will.

Thank You, Father, for the greatest blessing of all, the salvation that comes through Your one and only Son, Jesus Christ, in whose name we pray. Amen.

Endnotes

1. www.creditcards.com/credit-card-news/credit-card-industry-facts-personal-debt-statistics-1276.php.
2. www.bankruptcyaction.com/USbankstats.htm.
3. www.dailyfinance.com/2011/02/24/florida-leads-nation-in-foreclosure-rate/.
4. www.nationalhomeless.org/factsheets/How_Many.html.
5. www.smartmarriages.com/cohabit.html.
6. www.nytimes.com/2000/02/15/health/study-finds-families-bypassing-marriage.html?src=pm.
7. www.barna.org/barna-update/article/15-familykids/42.
8. www.whitehouse.gov/the_press_office/Joint-Press-Availability-With-President-Obama-And-President-Gul-Of-Turkey.
9. www.sojo.net/index.cfm?NewsID=5454&action=news.display_article&mode=C.
10. http://millercenter.org/president/speeches/detail/3446.
11. Arthur T. Pierson, *George Müller of Bristol and His Witness to a Prayer-Hearing God* (Charleston, SC: Nabu Press, 2011), 367.
12. www.ccc.org/WeBelieve/prayerofrepentance.html.
13. www.americananglican.org/general-convention-day-1-report-from-the-aac/.
14. Ibid.
15. George Barna, *The Second Coming of the Church* (Nashville: Word Publishing, 1998), 7–8.
16. Ibid., 6.
17. Ibid.
18. www.christianpost.com/news/38539.
19. www.barna.org/faith-spirituality/504.
20. www.barna.org/faith-spirituality/506.
21. http://pewforum.org/Age/Religion-Among-the-Millennials.aspx#attendance.
22. Andreas J. Köstenberger, *God, Marriage, and Family* (Wheaton, IL: Crossway Books, 2004), 25–26.
23. www.barna.org/family-kids-articles/42.
24. Ibid.
25. www.soundvision.com/Info/teens/stat.asp.

26. http://faithandfamily.com/radio/program/a-nation-in-peril/.

27. www.cdc.gov/mmwr/preview/mmwrhtml/mm5635a2.htm.

28. www.horicon.k12.wi.us/cms_files/resources/CASA%20 Parent%20Study%20Hands%20On-Hands%20Off%20Parents. pdf.

29. Nick Stinnett and John DeFrain, *Secrets of Strong Families* (Boston: Little, Brown and Company, 1986), 56.

30. www.barna.org/barna-update/article/15-familykids/106.

31. Ibid.

32. Ibid.

33. From a poem written in 1922 by Rhea F. Miller, with music added by George Beverly Shea.

34. www.cbsnews.com/8301-503544_162-20019931-503544.html.

35. www.cbo.gov/doc.cfm?index=12039.

36. C. S. Lewis, *Mere Christianity* (San Francisco: HarperSanFrancisco, 2001), 86.

37. W. A. Criswell, *Criswell's Guidebook for Pastors* (Nashville: B&H Books, 2000), 154.

About the Author

Henry Fernandez, inspirational speaker, author, and entrepreneur, is known for his practical, dynamic Bible teaching. With a prophetic message that cuts across denominational, cultural, and economic barriers, Fernandez is senior pastor of The Faith Center Ministries— a thriving multiracial congregation of over eight thousand people in Fort Lauderdale, Florida. He is also seen weekly on the Word Network and the Trinity Broadcasting Network.

A visionary who believes it is God's will for everyone to prosper and be in good health, Fernandez is committed to helping educate people as to what God's Word says about living and walking in victory. That commitment was demonstrated in part through his founding of the University of Fort Lauderdale, a fully accredited, nondenominational Christian institute approved by the Commission for Independent Education. The university, which was established to advance Christian education and promote leadership in secular and faith-based arenas alike, offers degrees at the associate, bachelor, master, and doctoral levels.

Fernandez' wife, Carol, serves as copastor of The Faith Center Ministries and often ministers alongside him at conferences, as well as at their home church. They are the parents of two sons, Seion-Zane and Elijah-Zane.